英語で雑談
できるようになる
生活フレーズ集

新崎 隆子
石黒 弓美子　著

研究社

まえがき

　本書は日本に住む人が外国の人に自分の生活について英語で話せるようになるための表現集です。初対面の外国人とごく普通の雑談が英語でできたらどんなにいいでしょうか。

　この本を書くきっかけは、スカイプによる英会話のレッスンを始めた30代の女性から悩みを打ち明けられたことでした。「毎朝出勤前に、30分ネイティブの先生と英語で話をしています。最初は難しかったですが、最近は挨拶やご機嫌伺い、天気や食べ物のことなど、無難な話題ならある程度話せるようになりました。でもその後が続かないのです。日本人の友人となら、もっといろんなことが話せるのに、英語で言おうとするとなんて言ったらいいか分からないことがあまりにも多くて」。

　日本で暮らしている人たちは日本語でものごとを考えます。生活の場面が英語圏ではないのですから外国人と英語を話す時でも「英語で考える」ことは基本的に無理です。ですから日本語で「うちは6人家族です」というようなメッセージを思いつきます。英語で言うとすれば"There are six people in my family." ですが、英語にはこういう発想がないので「こんなふうな言い方はしない」と言われてしまうかもしれません。でも、どんな言語でも自分の言いたいことが言えてこそ話す意味があるのです。ましてや、英語は世界の言語。異なる言語を母語とする多くの人たちが英語を使って活発に交流している時代です。日本にしかない「介護保険」などの制度や「墓参り」などの習慣についても、聞いた人に通じる限り、言いたいことはどんどん言えばいいと思います。

本書で紹介している例文の特徴は、本場仕込みのカジュアルな言い回しではなく、日本で英語を勉強してきた人たちにとって使いやすいものだということです。いくらカッコイイ表現でも、日本語の発想で捉えにくいものはなかなか真似することはできません。もうひとつは、自分のことを言うのに必要な表現を中心に選んでいることです。日本社会や日本文化を外国人に紹介するような「他人ごと」ではなく、ありのままの自分を語るために一人称 "I" で始める例文を集めるように心がけました。

　本書を使って仕事、結婚、子育て、外食、レジャー、人づきあいなど、日本での暮らしの様々な事柄について、英語で自分の言いたいことをどんどん話してください。

2016 年 6 月

新崎隆子

石黒弓美子

目次 Contents

まえがき iii

Chapter 1
日常生活を送る Everyday Life 001

No. 01 起きる・寝る 002

No. 02 身だしなみを整える 004

No. 03 食事をとる 006
1. 毎日の食事 006
   昼食に誘う 007
   お弁当に誘う 008
2. 自炊する 008
3. 買い出しに行く 009
   料理の作り方を説明する 011

No. 04 洗濯する 012

No. 05 掃除をする 015
1. 掃除をする 015
   掃除の種類 016
2. ゴミを出す 017
   ゴミの種類 018

No. 06 家計を管理する 019
1. 家計を管理する 019
   生活費の項目 021

2. 税金を払う 022
   保険の種類 023
3. 消費者金融を使う 023

No. 07 家族と暮らす 024
1. 家族について説明する 024
2. 結婚生活について話す 025
3. 家族の行事をおこなう 027
4. 子どもが結婚する 029
5. 家族の介護をする 029
6. 家族を看取る 030

No. 08 子育てする 031
1. 子どもが生まれる 031
2. 子どもの世話をする 032
3. 保育園に預ける 034
   職場から保育園のお迎えに行く 035
4. 育児に協力する 036

- 5. 子どもを学校に通わせる ...036
- 6. 塾や習い事に通わせる ...038
- 7. 大学を受験させる・浪人させる ...039

No.09 健康を管理する ...040
- 1. 定期健診を受ける ...040
  - 乳がん ...041
- 2. 健康状態について話す ...041
- 3. 治療を受ける ...043
- 4. 生活習慣を改善する ...044
- 5. 禁煙する・喫煙する ...045

No.10 住む ...046
- 1. 部屋を借りる・引っ越す ...046
- 2. 家賃を払う ...048
- 3. 家を買う ...049
  - 建ぺい率 ...050
- 4. 住宅ローンを組む ...050
- 5. 車を買う ...051

No.11 災害に備える ...053
- 1. 災害情報をチェックする ...053
- 2. 災害に備える ...054
- 3. 災害に遭う ...055
- 4. 事件や事故に遭遇する ...056
- 5. 火事が発生する ...057

No.12 動物や植物の世話をする ...059
- 1. ペットを飼う ...059
- 2. 魚を飼う ...060
  - 地域猫 ...061
- 3. 植物の世話をする ...061

No.13 人と付き合う ...063
- 1. 恋愛する ...063
- 2. 出会いを求める ...064
- 3. 断る ...064
- 4. 結婚する ...065
- 5. 結婚式をする ...065
- 6. 結婚後の展望を語る ...066
  - 両親にあいさつする ...068
- 7. 離婚する ...068
  - ハーグ条約 ...070

No.14 冠婚葬祭 ...071
- 1. 結婚式に出席する ...071
  - お祝儀を贈る ...072
- 2. 葬儀に参列する ...073
  - 葬儀に関する習慣 ...074
  - 葬儀の告知 ...075

No.15 行事やイベントを楽しむ ...076
- 1. 正月 ...076
  - おせち・お雑煮 ...078
  - 福袋 ...078
  - お年玉 ...079
- 2. バレンタインデー ...080
  - 義理チョコを渡す ...081
- 3. ホワイトデー ...082

- 4. ひな祭り ... 082
- 5. 子どもの日 ... 083
- 6. ゴールデン・ウィーク（5月の大型連休） ... 084
- 7. 七夕 ... 085
- 8. 夏休み ... 086
- 9. お盆 ... 087
- 10. 敬老の日 ... 087
- 11. 運動会 ... 088
  - 運動会の競技 ... 088
- 12. クリスマス ... 089
- 13. 大みそか ... 090
- 14. オリンピック ... 092
- 15. サッカーワールドカップ ... 093

No.16 日本の四季について話す ... 095
- 1. 春 ... 095
- 2. 花粉症 ... 096
- 3. 梅雨 ... 096
- 4. 夏 ... 097
  - 土用の丑の日 ... 098
- 5. 秋 ... 098
- 6. 冬 ... 099

Chapter 2
働く Work ... 101

No.01 仕事を志望する ... 102
No.02 就職活動をする ... 104
- 1. 就職活動をする ... 104
  - 売り手市場・買い手市場 ... 105
- 2. 就職のための勉強をする ... 105

No.03 自分の仕事について話す ... 107
- 1. 事務職 ... 107
  - お茶くみ ... 108
- 2. 経理 ... 109
- 3. 公務員 ... 109
- 4. コールセンターで働く ... 110
- 5. シフト勤務 ... 111
- 6. エンジニア ... 111
- 7. 営業の仕事 ... 112
- 8. 教育にかかわる仕事 ... 113
- 9. 派遣・パートで仕事をする ... 115

No.04 職場について話す ... 116
- 1. 会社について話す ... 116
- 2. 上司や同僚について話す ... 118
  - コピーを頼む ... 119
- 3. 歓送迎会・社員旅行 ... 119

No.05 転職する ... 121
No.06 退職する ... 124
- 1. 事情があって退職する ... 124

- 2. 会社が倒産する ... 126
- 3. 再就職する ... 126
  - 嘱託で働く ... 127

No.07 労働条件・福利厚生を調べる ... 128
- 1. 賃金について聞く ... 128
- 2. 労働時間について聞く ... 129
- 3. 福利厚生について聞く ... 130
- 4. 過労死の問題 ... 133

No.08 昇給する ... 134

No.09 出世する ... 136
- 総合職と一般職 ... 137

No.10 通勤する ... 138
- 1. 通勤時間 ... 138
- 2. 電車で通勤する ... 138
- 3. 電車が止まる・遅れる ... 140

No.11 接待する ... 141
- 1. 接待する ... 141
- 2. 食事に気を配る ... 142
  - 接待に関するやりとり ... 143

Chapter 3
自分の時間を過ごす　Free time ... 145

No.01 外食をする ... 146
- 1. レストランに行く ... 146
- 2. ファーストフード・ファミレスに行く ... 147
- 3. 居酒屋に行く ... 148
  - 飲みに誘う ... 149
- 4. 喫茶店に入る ... 150

No.02 ショッピングをする ... 151
- 1. 店で買い物をする ... 151
- 2. ネットショッピングをする ... 152

No.03 出かける ... 154
- 1. 旅行に行く ... 154
- 2. テーマパークに行く ... 156
- 3. 映画を観る ... 156
- 4. カラオケに行く ... 157
  - 遊びに誘う ... 158
- 5. スポーツ観戦に行く ... 159
- 6. 美容院・理髪店に行く ... 159

No.04 趣味を楽しむ ... 161
- 1. 音楽を楽しむ ... 161
- 2. 絵画を楽しむ ... 162
- 3. 手芸をする ... 163
- 4. 習い事をする ... 164
  - 生け花 ... 164
  - 茶道 ... 165

No.05 勉強する	166
1. 進学する	166
2. 英語を学ぶ	168
3. 英語の試験を受ける	169
4. 外国語を学ぶ	170
5. 運転免許をとる	171
6. 留学する	172
7. 会社の留学制度を利用する	174
8. 大学に再び通う・博士号を取得する	175
再入学・仮面浪人	176
9. 生涯学習で見識を高める	177

No.06 情報を収集する	178
1. インターネットを活用する	178
インターネットの問題点	179
2. スマホやタブレットを使う	179
3. LINE・ツイッターを利用する	181
4. 本を読む	182
5. テレビを観る	183
6. 新聞を取る	184

No.07 社会に参加する	185
1. 投票に行く	185
2. 祭りに参加する	186
3. 社会奉仕をする	186
4. 政治活動をする	187

No.08 スポーツを楽しむ	188
1. テニスをする	188
2. ゴルフをする	189
3. スキー・スノーボードをする	190
4. スキューバダイビングをする	191

Chapter 4
基本フレーズ Basic phrases ... 193

自己紹介をする	194
1. 名前	194
2. ○○出身[所属]です	194
3. 星座	195
星座の言い方	196
4. 干支	197
十二支	197

日本語索引 ... 198

Chapter 1

日常生活を送る

Everyday Life

起きてから寝るまで、
日常生活のあれこれを
英語で表現してみませんか?

No. 01

Chapter 1 Everyday Life

起きる・寝る

Getting up / Sleeping

01 朝7時ぴったりに目が覚めます。
I wake up at exactly 7 a.m.

---

02 寝起きが悪いです。
I have trouble getting up.

Note:「朝は機嫌が悪い」の意味では I'm grumpy in the morning.

---

03 よく二度寝をします。
After waking up, I often go back to sleep.

---

04 目覚まし時計のスヌーズを何回も止めます。
I hit the snooze button on my alarm clock again and again.

---

05 二度寝をして2時間が過ぎてしまい、会社に遅刻しました。
I was late for work because I went back to sleep and woke up two hours later.

---

06 毎晩寝る前には風呂に入ります。
I take a bath before going to bed every night.

---

07 寝つきが悪いです。
I have trouble falling asleep.

08 睡眠薬を飲んでいます。
I use sleeping pills.

---

09 手足が冷たくて眠れません。
I can't sleep well, because my hands and feet are cold.

---

10 休日に寝だめをします。
I catch up on sleep on my days off.

Note：「休日」（＝仕事が休みの日）の意味では、day off を使うのが一般的。

---

11 あと1時間は寝たいです。
I always wish I could sleep for another hour.

No. 02

Chapter 1　Everyday Life

身だしなみを整える
Getting ready

01 朝食前に顔を洗います。
I wash my face before breakfast.

02 何か食べたら歯を磨きます。
I brush my teeth after eating.

03 今朝はひげをそるのを忘れました。
I forgot to shave this morning.

Note : forget ～ ing = ～したのを忘れる／ forget to do= ～するのを忘れる

04 シャンプーをしたのにリンスをするのを忘れてしまいました。
I shampooed my hair but forgot to use conditioner.

05 朝はよくトイレがふさがっています。
The bathroom is busy in the morning.

06 寒くなったので厚手の上着を着ました。
I felt chilly and put on a heavy jacket.

07 何かはおるものを持って行った方がいいですよ。
You should bring something warm to wear.

08 夫には毎日下着を替えるように言っています。
I ask my husband to change his underwear every day.

09 息子にネクタイの結び方を教えました。
I taught [showed] my son how to put on a tie.

10 息子は服のコーディネートが上手です。
My son dresses well. / My son is a good dresser.

No. 03

Chapter 1　Everyday Life

食事をとる

Having a meal

1. 毎日の食事

01 朝食は時間がないのでいつもトーストとコーヒーです。
I'm busy in the morning. I usually have toast and coffee for breakfast.

Note：焼いた食パンは toast. bread は焼いていない素のパンを想像させる。デニッシュなどの菓子パンは pastries.

---

02 娘の朝食にパンを用意し、私たちはご飯とみそ汁を食べます。
I prepare toast for my daughter, while we have steamed rice and miso-soup.

---

03 お昼は会社にお弁当を持参します。
I take a box lunch [a *bento*] to work. / I take my lunch to work.

---

04 お昼は社員食堂でとります。
I have lunch at my company cafeteria.

---

05 お昼は友達と学食でとります。
I have lunch at the school cafeteria with my friends.

---

06 近所のお店にランチに行きます。
I have lunch at a restaurant nearby.

07 夜はコンビニで何か買って済ませます。
I buy something for dinner at a convenience store.

---

08 毎晩欠かさず晩酌をします。
I never have dinner without a drink.

---

09 週に1回、休肝日をもうけています。
I have one alcohol-free day every week to let my liver rest.

---

10 息子は好き嫌いが多いです。
There are so many things my son doesn't like to eat.

---

11 いそがしいのでついつい外食が多くなります。
I am very busy at work and often end up eating out quite frequently.

---

12 外食はお金がかかります。
It is expensive to eat out.

---

13 外食はどこも同じような味に感じられ、飽きてきます。
Restaurant food all starts to taste the same, so you [I] get tired of it.

Note : ⇒ p. 146「外食をする」

昼食に誘う

A： 昼休み、外に出ない？
Do you want to go out for lunch? / Why don't we go out for lunch?

03 食事をとる

B： いいよ。どこがいい？
Sure! Where do you want to go?

A： いいところ知ってる？
Do you know a good place to eat?

B： 近くに新しいレストランができたんで、行ってみない？
A new restaurant opened nearby. (Do you) Want to try it?

お弁当に誘う

ランチを作って来たので、一緒にどうですか。
I brought a homemade lunch. Do you want to join me?

多めに作って来たんですよ。
I prepared more food than I can eat all by myself.

> Note：home-made とも書くが、homemade と1つの単語としてつづることも多い。

2. 自炊する

01 最近は、自炊するようにしています。

These days I'm trying to cook meals at home.

> Note：「最近」は these days. nowadays は過去と比較する文脈で使われる。
> 例）Nowadays, Japanese women rarely wear kimonos.

---

02 私の好きな料理はグリルチキンです。

My favorite food is grilled chicken.

> Note：⇒ p.11「料理の作り方を説明する」

---

03 料理が好きなので、妻と一緒に台所にも立ちます。

I like cooking, so I sometimes cook with my wife.

04 実家が大家族だったので、つい大目に料理を作ってしまいます。
I'm from a big family, so I tend to cook much more than I can eat.

---

05 作った料理は小分けにして冷凍用の袋［ジップロック］に入れ冷凍にしておきます。
I divide the food I cook into smaller portions and freeze them in freezer bags [Ziploc bags].

---

06 残った料理を翌日のお弁当に持って行くこともあります。
Sometimes, I take leftovers for lunch the next day.

---

07 食べ物が無駄にならず、簡単にお弁当が作れるので便利です。
You don't let the food go to waste, and it's a convenient way to make a box lunch.

---

08 娘がテーブルの後かたづけをします。
My daughter cleans up and wipes the table.

---

09 食器洗いは私がします。
I usually do the dishes.

---

10 うちには食器洗い機があります。
We have a dishwasher.

---

3. 買い出しに行く

01 毎日、夕方5時ごろにスーパーに買い物に行きます。
I go shopping at the supermarket around 5 in the afternoon every day.

02 会社帰りに食材を買って帰ります。
I buy groceries on my way home from work.

---

03 私は日曜日に一週間分の買い物をします。
I buy a week's worth of groceries every Sunday.

---

04 一週間分の献立を考えておきます。
I plan a weekly menu.

---

05 チラシをチェックして少しでも安い店に行きます。
I choose the cheapest store by checking fliers [circulars].

Note：チラシは flier, 広告でいっぱいの flier は circular ともいう。

---

06 レジ袋はなるべく使わないようにしています。
I try not to use plastic bags whenever possible.

---

07 レジ袋を有料化する店が増えています。
More shops are now charging for plastic (grocery) bags.

---

08 私はエコバッグを持っていきます。
I bring an eco-friendly reusable bag.

---

09 バターが不足して品薄になり、値段も上がっています。
There's a butter shortage, and the price is going up.

---

10 バターの生産量が減って店に出回らず、値段が上がりました。
The production of butter has shrunk. Stores are short of butter and have increased its price.

料理の作り方を説明する

1. 鶏の手羽先の水気をペーパータオルで取ります。
   Pat the chicken wings dry with paper towels.

2. 余分な油を切ります。
   Shake off any excess oil from them.

3. 塩と胡椒を振ります。
   Sprinkle with salt and pepper.

4. オーブンに入れます。
   Put them into the oven.

5. 外がきつね色になるまで焼きます。
   Bake them until golden-brown on the outside.

6. 両側に醤油を刷毛で塗り、表面を軽く焦がします。
   Brush them on both sides with the soy sauce and bake until the glaze sizzles.

7. ニンジンの皮をむいて小さなサイコロ状に切ります。
   Peel and dice the carrot.

8. 塩を加えたお湯で2分間茹でます。
   Put them in salted boiling water for 2 minutes.

9. 醤油、砂糖、酒を小さなボールに入れて、砂糖が溶けるまで混ぜます。
   Mix soy sauce, sugar and *sake* in a small bowl until the sugar dissolves completely.

10. お皿に盛りつけましょう。
    Arrange them on the plates.

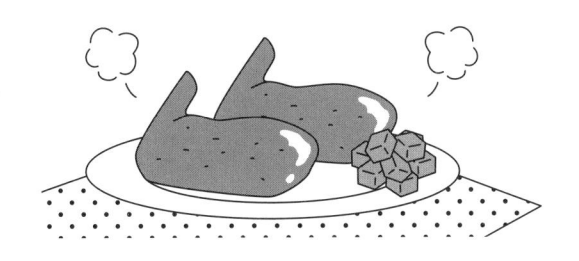

No. 04

Chapter 1 Everyday Life

洗濯する

Laundry

01 私は毎朝、出勤前に洗濯をします。
I do the laundry every morning before I go to work.

02 夕食後に洗濯物をたたみます。
I fold the laundry after dinner.

03 洗濯物はベランダに干します。
I hang out the washing on the balcony.

Note：日本語の「ベランダ」はしばしば英語の balcony. veranda は地上階にあるものを指す。

04 全自動洗濯機を買いました。
I bought a fully automatic washing machine.

05 アイロンがけは苦手です。
I'm not good at ironing.

06 クリーニング店の翌日配達サービスを利用しています。
I use the (dry) cleaner's next-day delivery service.

07 ワイシャツはノーアイロンのものしか着ません。
I wear permanent-press shirts only.

08 浴室乾燥機をつけるようにお勧めします。

I advise you to buy a bathroom dryer.

Note：一般的に浴室乾燥機が使われるのは日本のみ。浴室に洗濯物を干す習慣のない人も多い。We hang laundry and dry it in the bathroom. などと説明しよう。

---

09 息子には洗濯機にパンツを裏返しに入れないようにいつも言っています。

I always ask my son not to turn his underpants inside out when he puts them into the washing machine.

---

10 このドラム式洗濯機なら洗濯から乾燥まですべて自動でやってくれます。

This drum-type washing machine automatically washes and dries clothes.

Note：ドラム式洗濯機は drum-type washing machine, また front-loading washing machine（前入れ式洗濯機）などとも呼ばれる。

---

11 洗濯の際に柔軟剤を使います。

I use a fabric conditioner [softener] when I wash clothes.

---

12 柔軟剤を使って服をふんわり仕上げるだけでなく香りも楽しみます。

Fabric conditioners make clothes soft and smell good.

---

13 洗濯機でニットを洗ったら縮んでしまいました。

I shrank some knitwear items by machine-washing them.

14 部屋干しでは洗濯物がにおいます。

Drying laundry indoors makes it smell musty.

Note：musty かびくさい。

---

15 梅雨の時期は洗濯物を外に干せないので憂鬱です。

The rainy season is depressing because I can't dry laundry outside.

No. 05

Chapter 1 Everyday Life

掃除をする

Cleaning

1. 掃除をする

01 この部屋は埃っぽいですね。
This room is dusty, isn't it?

02 うちは月に2回お掃除サービスを利用しています。
We use a house cleaning service twice a month.

03 お掃除ロボットは便利ですが、その掃除が面倒です。
A cleaning robot is very convenient, but cleaning the robot is a pain.

04 子どもたちが泥足で家に入ってくると、玄関の床掃除をしなければいけません。
When my children come home with muddy feet, I have to clean the entrance floor.

05 晴れたので布団を干しました。
It was sunny, so I aired my *futon* (bedding) in the sun.

06 ダニやダニの死骸などアレルギー物質を取り除くために、布団にさっと掃除機をかけます。

I vacuum my *futon* lightly to remove allergens, such as living or dead dust mites.

Note:「アレルギーの原因」のような文脈で言う「ダニ」は dust mites と呼ばれる。

---

07 たまにエアコンのフィルターを掃除しなければなりません。

I need to clean air conditioner filters from time to time.

---

08 家の窓が結露します [＝空気中の水蒸気が窓ガラスに凝集します]。

The water vapor in the air condenses on the cold windowpanes in my house.

---

09 窓に水滴が垂れているのに気が付くたびに窓を拭きます。

I clean [wipe] the window every time I find condensation on the windowpane.

Note:「(窓などの) 結露」は condensation.

掃除の種類

■一般的な掃除 **clean;** 大掃除をする **give the house a thorough cleaning**

■掃き掃除 **sweep**
☞パートナーが掃き掃除をします。
My partner will do the sweeping.

■拭き掃除 **wipe;** (ごしごしこする) **scrub**

■モップをかける **mop**
☞あとで廊下にモップ掛けをしておきます。
I will mop the hallway later.

■はたきがけをする **dust**
☞ テレビにはたきをかけて下さい。
Dust the TV set, would you?

■掃除機をかける **vacuum**
☞ この部屋に掃除機をかけます。
I'll vacuum this room.

> Note：日本で年末に行う「大掃除」にあたるのは、春に行われる spring cleaning.
> 「(春の) 大掃除をする」は do spring cleaning.

2. ゴミを出す

01 可燃ゴミの収集は月曜日と金曜日です。
Burnable waste is collected on Mondays and Fridays.

02 水曜日は燃えないゴミの日です。
Wednesday is garbage collection day for non-burnables.

03 マンションに専有のゴミ捨て場があり、いつでもゴミを出せます。
I can take garbage to the collection site of my condominium anytime.

04 朝決まった時間にゴミを収集所に持っていきます。
I take garbage out to the collection site at a set time in the morning.

05 粗大ゴミを捨てる際には、事前に連絡が必要です。
When I want to throw away large items, I need to call a service for large trash pickup.

ゴミの種類

- 生ゴミ **garbage**
- 燃える[燃えない]ゴミ **burnable [non-burnable] garbage [trash]**
- 資源ゴミ **recyclable waste / recyclables**
- 粗大ゴミ **bulky trash [rubbish], large trash**

No. 06 Chapter 1 Everyday Life

家計を管理する
Managing the family budget

1. 家計を管理する

01 今月は黒字［赤字］でした。
We were in the black [red] this month.

02 月末が近づくといつもお金が足りなくなります。
I run out of money toward the end of the month.

03 収入の範囲で暮らすのはとても難しいです。
I have great difficulty (in) making (both) ends meet.

04 給料が低くて残業代がないと生活できません。
My salary is low. I can't make ends meet without overtime pay.

05 家計簿をつけています。
I'm keeping track of our household expenses.

06 妻が家計をすべて管理しています。
My wife manages our family budget.

07 ボーナスは全部貯金します。
I will save my entire bonus.

08 住宅ローンは2年前に完済しました。
I paid off the mortgage two years ago.

---

09 毎月の予算を決めて生活しています。
I plan a monthly budget to manage spending.

---

10 今月も食費が予算をオーバーしました。
I overspent on food items again this month.

---

11 毎月、奨学金を返しています。
I have to make a payment on my student loan every month.

> Note：日本で言う「(返済が必要な) 奨学金」は scholarship ではなく student loan（学生ローン）。

---

12 食品の値上げが続いています。
Food prices are going up and up.

---

13 給料は上がりません。
I don't get a pay raise.

---

14 別れた妻に養育費を払っています。
I pay child support to my ex-wife.

---

15 暗証番号を3回間違えたら、ATMからカードが出てきませんでした。
I put in the wrong PIN number three times, and then the ATM ate my card.

> Note：「間違った番号」は **the** wrong number.「間違った番号」は無数にあるはずだが、定冠詞 the を用いる。

16 公共料金を自動引き落としにしています。
I set up automatic payments for utilities.

---

17 ガス料金の引き落としができず、とうとうガスを止められました。
I didn't have enough money in my bank account to automatically pay my gas bill. Finally, they cut off my gas.

Note：⇒ p.22「税金を払う」

生活費の項目
- 食費 food expenses
- 光熱費 fuel and lighting expenses / energy expenses
- 住宅費 housing expenses
- 交際費 entertainment expenses
- 交通費 transportation expenses
- 娯楽費 recreation expenses
- 医療費 fees for medical treatment / medical expenses
- 通信費 communication expenses

2. 税金を払う

01 来年から消費税率が上がります。
The consumption tax rate will go up next year.

02 会社に勤めていると所得税は給料から天引きされます。
If you are a company employee, income tax is withheld from your salary.

Income tax is withheld from the salary of all company employees.

03 税金のほかに厚生年金の保険料や雇用保険料も給料から天引きされています。
In addition to tax, the public pension premium and employment insurance premium are also deducted from the employees' pay.

04 私は個人事業主なので、税務申告をしなければいけません。
I am a business owner. I have to report my income to the taxation office.

05 所得申告のために領収書をすべて取ってあります。
I keep all receipts to file my tax return.

06 額面賃金と手取り賃金の差に驚きます。
The difference between gross and net pay is amazing.

07 商品の税込表示と税抜表示が混在しています。
Merchandise prices are displayed as pre-tax or after-tax.

08 生命保険料などを支払った場合、一定額の所得控除を受けることができます。

I can get my life insurance premium deducted from my taxable income.

保険の種類

- 旅行保険 **travel insurance**
- 旅行傷害保険 **travel accident insurance**
- 健康保険 **health insurance**
- 医療保険 **medical insurance**
- 火災保険 **fire insurance**
- 生命保険 **life insurance**
- 自動車保険 **car insurance / auto(mobile) insurance / motor insurance / vehicle insurance**

3. 消費者金融を使う

01 買いたいものがあるけれどお金が足りないときは、10万円ぐらいまでなら消費者金融から借ります。

When I don't have enough money to buy something I want, if it's less than 100 thousand yen, I take out a consumer loan.

---

02 父はいつも、サラ金からお金を借りてはいけないと言っています。

My father always warns me not to take out a payday loan [borrow money from a payday lender].

> Note:「サラ金」は payday lender / payday loan. 非合法の「ヤミ金」は loan shark.「ヤミ金に手を出す」は borrow money from a loan shark.

No. 07

Chapter 1 Everyday Life

家族と暮らす

Family life

1. 家族について説明する

01 6人家族です。
There are six people in my family.

02 私は一人っ子です。
I'm an only child.

03 私は一人暮らしです(自活しています)。
I live by myself. / I live on my own.

04 私は独身です。
I'm not married.

05 私は同性のパートナーと暮らしています。
I'm living with my (same-sex) partner.

Note：単に partner と言っても通じる。会話の場合には、女性なら "I'm living with my girlfriend." 男性なら "I'm living with my boyfriend." などと言ってもよいだろう。

06 親は離婚しています。
My parents are divorced.

07 父は私が5つのときに亡くなりました。
I lost my father when I was five years old.

08 夏休みで娘が大学から帰省しています。
Our daughter is home from college for summer vacation.

---

09 兄とわたしはぜんぜん似ていないんです。
My brother and I do not look alike at all.

---

10 父は銀行勤めで、私たち家族はずっと引越しをし続けてきました。
My father works for a bank and my family has been moving from place to place all my life.

---

2. 結婚生活について話す

01 (子どもが独立したあと) 夫婦二人で暮らしています。
(My kids are grown, and) My husband and I are empty nesters.

Note：empty nester（子どもが巣立って）空の巣の人。

---

02 まだ子どもは作りません。
I don't want to have any children yet.

---

03 専業で家事をしています。
I am a housekeeper.

---

04 共働きです。
Both my husband [wife] and I work (for living).

---

05 家事は分担しています。
My husband [wife] and I share the housework.

06 夫はちっとも家事をしません。
My husband doesn't help a bit around the house.

---

07 夫は自分の仕事については、ほとんど何も話しません。
My husband tells me hardly anything about his job.

---

08 妻は私が働き過ぎだと考えています。
My wife thinks I'm working too hard.

---

09 妻の実家は北海道です。
My wife's parents live in Hokkaido.

---

10 年に 2, 3 回妻の地元に帰省します。
We go back to my wife's hometown two or three times a year.

---

11 妻の誕生日に何か良いものを贈りたいと思っています。
I want to find a really nice gift for my wife's birthday.

---

12 妻を素敵なプレゼントで驚かせたいと思っているんです。
I want to surprise my wife with a nice gift.

Note : ⇒ p.65「結婚する」

3. 家族の行事をおこなう

01 今度の土曜日には、娘の3歳の誕生日を祝います。
We will celebrate our daughter's 3rd birthday on Saturday.

02 明日は娘の初宮参りです。
Tomorrow we are taking our daughter to a shrine for the first time to pray for her life-long health and happiness.

03 息子が生まれて100日になるので、今週末は息子のお食い初めをします。
Our son will be 100 days old, so this weekend we'll have the "first meal" ritual to pray that he is happy and never goes hungry.

04 今度の土曜日には、娘のバレエの発表会に行きます。
We'll be going to our daughter's ballet performance on Saturday.

05 毎週日曜日、息子の野球［サッカー］の試合を見に行きます。
We go to our son's baseball game [soccer match] every Sunday.

06 8月半ばのお盆には帰郷し、墓参りに行きます。
We will go to our hometown in mid-August for the *Bon* festival and to visit the family grave to pay homage to our ancestors.

Note：個人の、または家族の墓（の一区画）は grave.（⇒ p.87「お盆」）

07 11月2日は我々の5年目の結婚記念日です。
November 2nd is our 5th (wedding) anniversary.

---

08 子どもをおばあちゃんに預けて、夫婦で食事に出ます。
We plan to leave our kids with their grandmother and go out to [for] a nice dinner.

---

09 12月3日は伯父の四十九日［三回忌］の法事に出席します。
On December 3rd, I'll be attending a memorial service for the 49-day [3-year] anniversary of our uncle's death.

---

10 子どもは皆独り立ちしましたので、妻とゆっくり旧婚旅行にでも行きます。
Our children are all independent now. I now would like to take my wife on a second honeymoon.

Note : ⇒ p.31「子育てする」

4. 子どもが結婚する

01 娘が今度結婚するんです。
Our daughter is getting married.

02 バージンロードを娘と歩くのは、ちょっと緊張します。
I feel a bit nervous about walking our daughter down the aisle.

Note：「バージンロードを娘と歩く」walk my daughter down **the aisle**.

03 娘を嫁にやるのは、複雑な気持ちです。
I have mixed feelings about our daughter's wedding.

04 娘の結婚式では、涙を見せたくはありませんね。
I would hate to show tears at our daughter's wedding.

5. 家族の介護をする

01 うちの両親は介護保険制度のサービスを利用しています。
My parents use services of the public nursing care system.

02 母は今日デイケアに行っています。
My mother is at the day-care center today.

03 要介護高齢者のためのショートステイサービスで、家族はほっとできます。
Short-stay service for frail elderly people gives relief for the family.

04 祖父は3カ月前に、やっと特別養護老人ホームに入れました。
My grandfather finally entered a special nursing care facility three months ago.

---

05 母は認知症です。
My mother is suffering from dementia [senility].

---

06 母は深夜に街を徘徊していたところを警察に保護されました。
My mother was found wandering around town in the middle of the night and taken into care by the police.

---

6. 家族を看取る

01 昨夜おそく父がなくなりました。
My [Our] father passed away late last night.

---

02 父は、92歳、大往生でした。
Our father died a peaceful death at the age of 92.

---

03 父は、ぴんぴんころりで逝きました。私もそうありたいです。
Our father was active until the day he died. That's the way I'd like to go.

---

04 父は長く患っていましたが、お陰様で、私たちはゆっくりと時間をかけて父と最後の日々を過ごすことができました。
We were happy that we could spend many days with him before we finally had to say good-bye to him, though he had to struggle with his illness for many years.

No. 08

Chapter 1　Everyday Life

子育てする

Raising children

1. 子どもが生まれる

01 妊娠しています。
I'm pregnant [expecting].

02 出産予定日は 10 月 1 日です。
The baby is due on October 1st.

03 妻はつわりで大変です。
My wife is suffering from morning sickness.

04 彼女は今妊娠 10 週です。
She is in her 10th week.

05 私は妊娠 2 ヶ月目で流産しました。
I miscarried when I was two months pregnant.

06 赤ちゃんは自然分娩［帝王切開］で生まれました。
My baby was born by natural delivery [by C-section / by Caesarean / by Cesarean].

07 分娩には 6 時間かかりました。
I was in labor for 6 hours.

08 2人目がもうすぐ生まれます。
Our second baby is on the way.

---

09 息子は20日ほど早産でしたが、無事育ちました。
I delivered my son about twenty days prematurely, but he developed normally [he grew up just fine].

---

10 妻は来月から半年の産休を取ります。
My wife will take a six-month maternity leave starting from next month.

---

11 子どもが生まれたら、私も1週間は育休を取るつもりです。
When the baby comes, I will also take a week off to stay with my family.

2. 子どもの世話をする

01 粉ミルクより母乳の方が健康に良いと聞いたので、母乳に決めました。
I decided to breast feed my baby because I hear it's healthier than formula feeding.

---

02 おむつかぶれができないように、ウンチをしたらできるだけ早くおむつを替えなければいけません。
I have to change her diaper as soon as possible after she poops to avoid diaper rash.

Note：poop, poo うんちをする。poop のほうがやや一般的。

---

03 一人で歩けるようになりました。
My baby can walk all by himself [herself] now.

04 おむつが取れました。
My son has finished potty training.

---

05 抱っこをいやがります。
My daughter doesn't like to be held.

---

06 娘はイヤイヤ期［恐るべき2歳］です。
My daughter is in her "terrible twos."

Note：第一次反抗期は2〜3歳で訪れることから。

---

07 つい子どもに怒鳴ってしまいます。
I can't help shouting at my children.

---

08 夫は、最初、生まれたばかりの赤ちゃんがあまりに小さく弱々しいのでちょっと怖気づいたと言います。
My husband says he was a bit scared in the beginning by how tiny and fragile our newborn baby was.

---

09 赤ちゃんをゆすると脳の出血を起こすかもしれないから絶対にやってはいけないと言われました。
I was told never to shake our baby because it can cause bleeding in the brain.

---

10 来週は、三種混合ワクチンの接種で［3カ月健診で］、娘をかかりつけの医者に連れて行きます。
We will take our daughter to her doctor for the DPT vaccine [shot] [for her three-month physical checkup].

Note：DPTは diphtheria-pertussis-tetanus（ジフテリア、百日咳、破傷風）

11 6歳の娘に妹をしっかり抱く方法を教えてあげました。

I told my 6-year-old daughter how to hold her younger sister properly.

---

12 4歳の娘は鬼ごっこが大好きですが、8歳の息子はコンピューターゲームに夢中です。

My 4-year-old daughter loves playing tag, but my 8-year-old son is (really) into computer games.

> Note : キャッチボール play catch ／かくれんぼ play hide and seek
> お手玉 juggle beanbags ／けん玉 play with a *kendama*
> 凧揚げ fly a kite.

---

3. 保育園に預ける

01 共働きなので、4月から娘は保育園にあずけます。

Since we both work, we will send our daughter to a day care starting in April.

---

02 子どもが熱を出すと保育園ではあずかってもらえないので大変です。

It's tough because our day care won't take kids when they have a fever.

---

03 子どもが病気のときは、妻か私のどちらかが仕事を休まなくてはなりません。

When our kids get sick, either my wife or I have to take a day off.

---

04 日々子どもの成長を見ることができるのはとても楽しいです。

It's really fun to watch our kids grow day by day.

05 この街には公立の保育園が足りません。

There is a shortage of public child care centers in this town.

---

06 共働きなので、子どもは保育園に預けています。

Both my wife [husband] and I work, and our son [daughter] goes to day care.

---

07 うちの会社にはフレックス制度があるので、朝は私が子どもを保育園に連れて行きます。

I work flexible hours, and I take our son [daughter] to day care in the morning.

---

08 妻が仕事帰りに子どもたちを保育園に迎えに行きます。

My wife picks our kids up in the afternoon on her way home.

職場から保育園のお迎えに行く

A： 悦子さん、もうお迎えの時間じゃないの。
その仕事やっておいてあげるから、早く帰って。

Etsuko, I think it's time for you to go and pick up your children. I'll finish what you are doing. So just hurry and go!

B： すみません！ 恩にきます。

Thank you so much! You're a big help!

じゃ。お先に失礼します。

Excuse me, then.

4. 育児に協力する

01 私が家に帰るころには、たいてい子どもは寝ています。
By the time I get back home, our son [daughter] is usually sleeping.

02 週末にはできるだけ子どもと一緒に遊ぶようにしています。
On weekends, I try to play with our son [daughter] as much as possible.

03 おむつも取り替えますし、風呂にも入れます。
I change his [her] diaper and give him [her] a bath, too.

04 ときどき遊園地など、子どもが喜びそうな所へ行ったりします。
Sometimes we take our kid to an amusement park or some other place he [she] might like.

Note：⇒ p.66「結婚後の展望を語る」

5. 子どもを学校に通わせる

01 4月には息子が小学校に入学します。
Our son will be starting elementary school in April.

Note：「入学する」は start school. enter school はあまり使われない。

02 3月の娘の中学校の卒業式には出たいと思っています。
I want to attend our daughter's graduation ceremony at her junior high school in March.

03 彼ら（子どもたち）のために十分な教育費を準備しておかなければなりません。

We have to save enough money for their education.

---

04 息子を私立の中高一貫校に入学させようと考えています。

I would like my son to go to a private school for junior high and (senior) high school.

---

05 娘は公立の中学校でのびのび過ごしてほしいと考えています。

I hope my daughter will enjoy herself at a public junior high school.

---

06 娘が希望する会社から内定の知らせがあり、喜んでいます。

We are happy that our daughter has gotten a job offer from a company she wants to work for.

---

07 うちの子どもたちにはいつももっと勉強しなさいと言っていますが、ちっとも聞いてくれません。

I always advise my children to study harder, but they won't listen to me.

---

08 娘は勉強もせずクラブ活動ばかり熱心です。

My daughter doesn't study. She's interested in nothing but her club activities.

---

09 娘から学校でいじめにあっていると聞いて心配です。

I'm worried because I heard my daughter is being bullied at school.

10 娘がアメリカの高校に留学したいと言うのですが、主人が強く反対しています。

Our daughter says she wants to go to senior high school in the United States, but my husband is strongly against the idea.

11 主人は娘に婚期を逃さないために大学院には行かないほうがいいと言いました。

My husband told our daughter that she'd better not go to graduate school, because she might miss a chance to get married.

すると娘は主人と口を聞かなくなりました。
She stopped talking to her father.

6. 塾や習い事に通わせる

01 息子はスイミングスクールに行っています。
My son is going to swimming school.

02 娘はピアノを習っています。
My daughter is taking piano lessons.

03 うちの子どもたちは週2回塾に行っています。
Our children go to cram school twice a week.

04 平日は、娘は学校から帰ると一人で夕食を食べて塾に向かいます。
On weekdays, our daughter comes home from school, has dinner by herself and goes to cram school.

7. 大学を受験させる・浪人させる

01 息子が来年大学を受験します。
My son will take entrance examinations for universities next year.

02 下の娘は受験に失敗して、予備校に通っています。
Our younger daughter failed her examinations, so she's going to prep [preparatory] school now.

03 娘は二浪してABC大学の経済学部に合格しました。
My daughter finally got into ABC University, Department of Economics, after she failed the entrance exam two years in a row.

04 息子が希望の大学に受かったのでホッとしています。
We are so happy that our son has passed the entrance examination to the university he wants to go to.

05 息子は推薦入試で高校3年生の秋に進路が決まりました。
In autumn of his senior year, our son was admitted to a university based on a recommendation.

Note：in autumn of one's senior year で「高校3年の秋」となる。

Note：⇒ p.166「進学する」

08 子育てする

No. 09   Chapter 1 Everyday Life

健康を管理する

Health care

1. 定期健診を受ける

01 私は毎年健診を受けています。
I get a checkup every year.

02 まず、身長と体重を量ります。
First, they check my height and weight.

03 そして血液検査と尿検査を受けます。
Then I have a blood test and a urine test.

04 胸部のレントゲン検査と胃カメラ検査もします。
I also have a chest X-ray and a gastroscopy.

05 昨年は腹部超音波検査で胆のうにポリープが見つかりました。
Last year, I was told that I had a polyp in my gallbladder after I had [underwent] an abdominal ultrasound.

06 精密検査を受けるように言われました。
I was told to undergo a thorough examination.

07 結果は異状なしでした。
I had no problems [abnormalities].

08 私は毎年病院で乳がんの検査をしています。
I go to the hospital for breast cancer screening every year.

09 私の住んでいる町では触診の検査は無料です。
In my town, a palpation test is free of charge.

10 マンモグラフィーの検査は有料ですが、2年に1度は受けています。
I have to pay for mammography, but I have [undergo] one every two years.

11 自分でも日常的に胸のしこりがないか調べています。
I also do routine breast exams myself.

乳がん

かつて日本における乳がん発症率は欧米を下回っていました。
The incidence of breast cancer in Japan was lower than in Western countries in the past.

最近は乳がんの発症率が年々増加し、今では日本人女性がかかるがんのトップです。
Recently, the incidence has increased year by year, and now breast cancer is the most common cancer for Japanese women.

---

2. 健康状態について話す

01 頭が痛い。
I have a headache.

02 寒気がします。
I have chills.

03 熱があります。
I have a fever.

04 食欲がありません。
I have no appetite.

05 咳がでます。
I have a cough.

06 昨日から湿疹があります。
I have had a rash since yesterday.

07 吐き気があります。
I feel sick (to my stomach).

08 ピーナッツアレルギーです。
I am allergic to peanuts.

09 今生理中です。
I'm having my period now.

10 夫は病的な肥満です。
My husband is morbidly obese.

11 インフルエンザにかかり、1週間安静にしていました。
I was in bed with the flu for a week.

12. ノロウイルスに感染し、一晩中トイレにこもっていました。
I came down with norovirus and suffered severe diarrhea. I was in the bathroom all night.

---

13. ぎっくり腰になりました。
I strained my back. / I put my back out.

---

14. 首を寝違えました。
I slept funny and got a crick in my neck.

---

15. 老眼がはじまりました。
I'm getting farsighted as I get older.

Note：婉曲に表現する場合は I'm old enough to need reading glasses.（年だから読書用のメガネが必要だ）。

---

3. 治療を受ける

01. 結膜炎で眼科にかかっています。
I am seeing an ophthalmologist for conjunctivitis.

---

02. 病院はどこも混んでいます。
Hospitals are crowded everywhere.

---

03. 父が胃潰瘍で入院しました。
My father was admitted to the hospital for a stomach ulcer.

---

04. 2週間で退院しました。
He left the hospital after two weeks.

09 健康を管理する

05 祖父が肺がんの手術をしました。
My grandfather underwent surgery for lung cancer.

06 妻はすぐ良くなりました。
My wife got well soon.

07 祖母は点滴をしています。
My grandmother is on an IV (drip).

Note：IV は intravenous（静脈注射、点滴）の略。

4. 生活習慣を改善する

01 私は週に2回スポーツジムにいきます。
I go to a gym twice a week.

02 今、ダイエット中です。
I'm on a diet.

03 夜9時以降は食べないようにしています。
I don't eat after 9 p.m.

04 エスカレーターではなく階段を使うようにしています。
I usually go up the stairs rather than take the escalator.

05 1日最低6時間は睡眠をとるようにしています。
I try to sleep for at least 6 hours every day.

06 寝不足だと会議中に居眠りしてしまいます。
When I don't get enough sleep, I sometimes doze off during meetings.

---

07 ドライアイに悩まされています。
I suffer from dry eyes.

---

08 スマートフォンを使いすぎないように気を付けています。
I try not to spend too much time on my smartphone.

5. 禁煙する・喫煙する

01 禁煙中です。
I've stopped smoking.

---

02 愛煙家で1日1箱は吸います。
I'm a heavy smoker. I smoke more than one pack a day.

Note：続けざまに吸うような人は chain-smoker（チェーンスモーカー）。

---

03 最近は嫌煙家が多くて肩身がせまいです。
I feel ashamed because many people hate smoking these days.

---

04 父はかつてヘビースモーカーでしたが、私が生まれて煙草をやめました。
My father used to be a heavy smoker, but he quit smoking after I was born.

No. 10

Chapter 1　Everyday Life

住む

Housing

1. 部屋を借りる・引っ越す

01 部屋を探していています。
I'm looking for an apartment.

Note：「（アパートなどの）部屋」は an apartment を使う。a room は誰かの家の中の一部屋を借りる（シェアする）ことを想像させる。

02 1DK のアパートを探しています。
I'm looking for a studio apartment [flat].

03 その部屋はまだ空いていますか？
Is the apartment still available?

04 お湯はガスです［電気です］。
The hot water is heated by gas [electricity].

05 日中の日当たりは良いです。
This apartment gets a lot of sun during the day.

06 新しいアパートの賃貸契約をしました。
I signed the lease for my apartment.

07 大家さんが保証会社を使うことを条件にしました。
The landlord required me to sign up with a guarantor company.

08 大家さんが保証人を要求しました。
The landlord required me to provide a private guarantor.

09 ペットを飼えるアパートを探しています。
I am looking for a pet-friendly apartment.

10 この辺りは治安がいい[悪い]です。
This area is safe [not safe].

11 オートロックのマンションに住みたいです。
I want to live in an apartment with a self-locking entrance.

12 押し売り業者に直接会わなくて済みますから。
Then I can avoid meeting aggressive sales people face to face.

13 トイレ風呂別の部屋に住みたいです。
I want an apartment with a separate toilet and bath.

14 風呂の追い炊き機能があるとよいのですが。
I'd like a bath with a reheating function.

15 バブルの時代に質の悪いマンションが大量に建てられました。
A huge number of poor quality condominiums were built during the bubble era.

2. 家賃を払う

01 家賃にインターネット代［電気代・ガス代］は含まれています。
Internet [Electricity / Gas] is included in the rent.

02 敷金は家賃2か月分です。
I have to pay a security deposit of two months' rent [pay a two-month security deposit].

03 礼金を1か月分払います。
I have to pay a nonrefundable one-time fee of one month's rent as key money.

04 不動産屋に手数料を払わなければなりません。
I have to pay a commission to the real estate agent.

05 ときには賃貸料に共用部分の掃除などの管理料金が含まれていることもあります。
In some cases, the rent includes a management fee for maintenance, including cleaning common areas.

06 住みやすい部屋は家賃が高いです。
A comfortable apartment is expensive (to rent).

07 家賃の相場は手取り給料の3分の1と言われています。
The average rent is said to be about one third of your salary after tax.

3. 家を買う

01 家を買う計画があるのなら、まず不動産屋に問い合わせをしましょう。
When you plan to buy a house, first you should contact a real-estate agent.

02 その地域の建ぺい率を調べておきましょう。
I advise you to check the legal building-to-land ratio in the area.

03 管理費や修繕積立金を調べておいた方がいいですよ。
You should check maintenance fees and contributions to the renovation fund.

04 建売住宅を買うときは、必ず建物の耐震性について尋ねましょう。
When you buy a house on a piece of land, don't forget to ask questions about earthquake proofing of the building.

05 私は一戸建てを買うのが夢でした。
It was my dream to buy a (detached) house.

06 私の好みはマンションです。
I prefer a condominium.

07 注文建築で家を建てました。
I bought land and asked a builder to construct the house.

08 都心にマンションを買いました。
I bought a condominium in the downtown area.

09 ゆくゆくはそのマンションを人に貸して家賃収入を得る予定です。

I plan to rent out the condominium to earn income in the future.

建ぺい率

1. 建ぺい率とは敷地面積に対する建築面積の割合のことです。
   "Kenpei-ritsu" means the building-to-land ratio.
2. 一般的に、建ぺい率が高ければ、土地に対してより広い家が建てられます。
   When the building-to-land ratio is high, you can build a larger house relative to the land area.

Note :「容積率」は a floor-area ratio（略：FAR）.

4. 住宅ローンを組む

01 どれぐらい銀行から借りられるかは、私の信用審査で決まります。

How much I can borrow from the bank depends on their evaluation of my credit.

---

02 月々の返済額はいくらになりますか。

What are the monthly payments?

---

03 住宅ローンの金利が低くなっていますので、家を買うなら今がチャンスです。

Mortgage rates are low now. It's a good time to buy a house.

---

04 ローンで家を購入する時、夫は団体信用生命保険に入りました。

My husband took out a creditor insurance policy when he got a loan to buy a house.

05 夫に万一のことがあっても、保険でローン残高が支払われます。
Even if the unthinkable [if something terrible] happens to my husband, repayment of the outstanding loan will be covered by the insurance.

06 住宅ローンを組むために夫には健康でいてもらわなければなりません。
Since we're taking out a mortgage, I need my husband to stay healthy.

5. 車を買う

01 車を買うときは車庫証明が必要です。
I have to verify that I have a parking space to buy a car.

02 新車の四輪駆動を買いました。
I bought a brand new 4WD [four wheel drive] vehicle.

03 地元のカーディーラーを紹介しましょう。
I will introduce you to a local car dealer.

04 強制保険だけでなく任意保険にも入った方がいいですよ。
I advise you to buy the optional vehicle insurance in addition to the mandatory liability insurance.

05 子どもが生まれたので、セダンからミニバンに変えました。
After we had a baby, we replaced our sedan with a minivan.

06 3人目の子どもができたのでキャンプ用自動車を買いました。
I bought a camper after we had our third child.

---

07 2年に一度の車検の費用も忘れてはいけません。
Keep in mind that you have to pay for mandatory car inspection every other year.

---

08 地方に住んでいるので、どこへ行くにも車が必要です。
I live in the countryside. I need a car to go anywhere.

---

09 お金がないので通勤用にスクーターを購入しました。
I don't have enough money to buy a car. I bought a scooter instead.

---

10 車で通勤しているので飲み会のときには家族に迎えに来てもらいます。
I go to work by car. I have to ask my family to pick me up when I go for a drink after work.

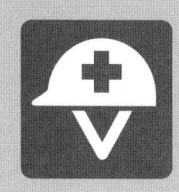

No. 11 災害に備える
Disaster prevention

Chapter 1 Everyday Life

1. 災害情報をチェックする

01 大型の台風が近づいているそうです。
I hear a powerful typhoon is approaching.

02 高潮警報がでたので、釣りはやめました。
I canceled fishing because a storm surge warning was issued.

03 うちの村には避難指示がでました。
Residents in our village have been ordered to evacuate.

04 土砂崩れの恐れがあります。
The risk of mudslides is high.

05 厳しい暑さが続きます。熱中症に気をつけなければいけません。
The scorching heat continues. We have to take steps to prevent heatstroke.

06 この地震による津波の恐れはありません。
There is no risk of tsunamis caused by this earthquake.

2. 災害に備える

01 このマンションは震度 5 の地震には耐えられる設計になっています。

This condominium is designed to withstand an earthquake of intensity 5 or stronger.

> Note:「震度 5」をより正確に表現する場合は、Intensity 5 of the Japanese scale from 0 to 7.

---

02 この病院は停電に備えて自家発電装置があります。

This hospital has a private power generator for use in case of power failure.

---

03 非常持ち出し袋は持っていますか。

Do you have an emergency kit?

---

04 この村には防災無線システムがあります。

This village has a radio communication system for disaster prevention.

---

05 全ての鉄道網に自動運転停止装置がついています。

The whole railway network is equipped with ATS [Automatic Train Stop].

---

06 家に 3 日分の食料を備蓄しています。

I store a three-day supply of food at home.

---

07 家具が転倒しないように突っ張り棒を設置しました。

I set up spring tension rods to prevent the furniture from falling over.

08 川では局所的な大雨がふり、急に増水したりしますから、油断は禁物です。

We should not be taken off guard by swollen river waters, which can be caused by a sudden localized heavy rainfall.

---

3. 災害に遭う

01 突風でうちの家の屋根が吹き飛びました。

A gust of wind blew off the roof of our house.

---

02 うちの家族は近くの小学校に避難しました。

Our family took shelter at an elementary school nearby.

---

03 あっという間に浸水の被害が広がりました。

The flood damage spread so fast.

---

04 30軒の家が壊れました。

Thirty houses were destroyed.

---

05 家の片付けに追われました。

We worked hard to tidy up our house.

---

06 みんなくたくたでした。

We were all exhausted.

---

07 私たちは川の中州に取り残されました。

We were stranded on a sandbar in the river.

08 遭難者はヘリコプターで救助されました。
Survivors were rescued by helicopter.

09 空港に到着したころには、全ての便が欠航になっていました。
When I arrived at the airport, all flights had been canceled.

10 鉄道会社が他の路線に振替輸送をしていました。
The railway company transferred passengers to other train services.

11 A駅とB駅の間で上下線とも運休しています。
The train services are suspended in both directions between A station and B station.

12 毎年大雪が降り、冬は雪かきに追われます。
We have heavy snow every year. We are busy shoveling the snow in winter.

13 毎年、ゲリラ豪雨によって人的被害が出ています。
Sudden torrential rain kills or injures people every year.

4. 事件や事故に遭遇する

01 昨夜、近所で交通事故がありました。
There was a traffic accident near my house last night.

> Note: 死亡事故 a fatal accident.
> 飲酒運転のドライバーによる事故 a drunk-driving accident.

Chapter 1

02 その事故で 5 人が死傷しました。
Five people were killed or injured in the accident.

---

03 幸い、死傷者は出ませんでした。
Fortunately, there were no casualties.

---

04 路上でひったくりの被害にあいました。
I had my bag snatched on the street.

---

05 バイクで近づいてきた男にハンドバッグを奪われました。
A man approached me by motorbike and snatched my handbag.

---

06 駅前のコンビニに強盗が押し入り、レジから売上金を奪いました。
Somebody broke into the convenience store in front of the station and stole the days' proceeds from the cash register.

---

07 犯人は捕まっていません。
The robber hasn't been arrested.

Note：犯人 criminal ／容疑者 suspect.

---

08 同級生が万引きで捕まりました。
A classmate of mine was caught shoplifting.

5. 火事が発生する

01 先週、木造住宅が全焼する火事がありました。
A wooden house burned down in a fire last week.

02 火は車庫から出ました。
The fire originated in the garage.

03 放火の疑いがあります。
They suspect arson.

No. 12　　　　　　　　　　　　　　　　Chapter 1　Everyday Life

動物や植物の世話をする
Caring for plants and animals

1. ペットを飼う

01 毎朝、犬を散歩させます。
I walk my dog every morning.

02 小型犬なので、部屋の中で飼っています。
It's a small dog, so I keep it in the house.

Note：賃貸の部屋なら in my apartment, 単に「屋内で」という場合は indoors.

03 このマンションを買ったのはペットの飼育が許されているからです。
I bought this condominium because residents are allowed to keep pets.

04 獣医さんのところで狂犬病の予防接種をしてもらいます。
I take my dog to a vet for his rabies shot.

05 旅行の間はペットホテルに預けます。
I board my dog at a kennel while I'm traveling.

06 ネコがソファーで爪をとぐので困っています。
I don't know what to do about my cat sharpening her claws on the sofa.

12　動物や植物の世話をする　　059

07 愛犬の桃太郎が 14 歳で死にました。
Our dog Momotaro died at the age of 14.

---

08 ペットロスから立ち直る方法はありませんか。
Do you have any tips on coping with pet loss?

---

09 2 年前から文鳥のつがいを飼っています。
I have had a pair of Java sparrows for two years.

---

10 ケージから出すと、部屋の中を飛び回って、ときどき私の肩に止まります。
When I release them from the cage, they fly around the room and sometimes perch on my shoulder.

---

11 捨て猫だったネコを引き取りました。
I took in a stray cat.

---

12 ペットの毛が抜けるので掃除が大変です。
It's hard to clean up all of the pet hair.

> Note: My pet sheds a lot and it's hard to clean up after him.（毛がたくさん抜けるので掃除が大変）とも。clean up after 〜：〜の後始末をする。

2. 魚を飼う

01 熱帯魚を飼おうと思って、水槽を買いました。
I bought an aquarium for tropical fish.

---

02 熱帯魚はただ餌をやればいいだけではありません。
To take good care of tropical fish, I have to do more than just feed them.

03 水を清潔に保ち水温の管理をしなければいけません。
I have to keep the water clean and warm enough.

地域猫

- 地域猫：**stray cats in the neighborhood**
  - たくさんの野良猫が地域に住み着いています。
    Lots of stray cats live in this area.
  - ボランティアが近所の野良猫の面倒を見ています。
    Volunteers care for the stray cats in our neighborhood.
  - 彼らは野良猫に避妊や去勢手術を受けさせます。
    They have stray cats spayed or neutered.

3. 植物の世話をする

01 ベランダ園芸を楽しんでいます。
It's fun to grow plants on a balcony.

---

02 夏は朝晩水をやらなければなりません。
I have to water them in the morning and in the evening every day during summer.

---

03 トマトやキュウリなどの野菜を育てています。
I grow vegetables, such as tomatoes and cucumbers.

04 観葉植物をもらいましたが、部屋が狭くて置くところがありません。

I was given a leafy, potted plant, but I can't find a place to put it in my small room.

---

05 背の高い木の剪定はプロに任せています。

I use a professional pruning service for the tall trees.

---

06 梅の木が毎年実をつけます。

Plum trees produce fruit every year.

---

07 収穫した梅で梅酒を漬けます。

I make plum wine with homegrown plums.

---

08 駅前で自分用のブーケを買って部屋に飾っています。

I bought myself a flower bouquet at a shop close to the station and put it in my room.

---

09 庭の雑草を取るのが大変です。

It's painstaking to weed the garden.

---

10 会社の机に小さな観葉植物を置いています。

I have a small potted plant on my desk in the office.

---

11 植物をすぐに枯らしてしまいます。

I'm not good at keeping plants alive.

> Note:「植物を育てるのが苦手です」と言う場合、have a green thumb（花や植物を育てるのがうまい）の逆、"I have a brown thumb." という言い方もある。

No. **13**

Chapter 1　Everyday Life

人と付き合う

Relationships

1. 恋愛する

01 付き合ってる人いるんですか。
Are you seeing anyone?

02 誰とも付き合っていません。
I'm not seeing anyone.

03 この間集団お見合いであった人と付き合っています。
I'm going with someone that I met through a matchmaking event.

04 インターネットのお見合いサイトで見つけた人と初めてデートします。
I'll be meeting someone I found on an online dating site for singles for the first time.

05 この間合コンで会った人と週末に美術館に行くんです。
I'm going to an art museum this weekend with a man [a woman] I met at a matchmaking party the other day.

06 彼とは、友達のパーティで会いました。
I met him at a party thrown by a friend of mine.

13　人と付き合う　　063

07 彼はちょっとかわいい人です。
He is kind of cute.

2. 出会いを求める

01 全く出会いがなくって。
I haven't met anyone at all.

02 お見合い結婚もアリかな。
I've started to think getting married through a matchmaker might be a possibility.

03 怪しげなお見合いサイトには騙されないよう気をつけたほうが良いです。
We should be very careful not to be tricked by any dubious matchmaking sites.

3. 断る

01 まだ結婚する気になれないんです。
I'm not ready to get married yet.

02 まだ誰とも結婚したいとは思っていません。
I'm not thinking about marrying anyone yet.

4. 結婚する

01 独身です。
I'm single.

02 婚約相手がいます。
I'm engaged.

03 ついに (結婚) 相手を見つけました。
I'm happy because I've finally met the right person.

04 僕たち今度結婚することになりました。
We are getting married.

05 できちゃった結婚なんです。
Actually, we are getting married because we found out that we are expecting a baby.

06 僕たちはバツイチですけど。別に気にしません。
We are both divorced. But we don't care.

Note:「彼は[彼女は]バツイチです」He's [She's] divorced.

5. 結婚式をする

01 結婚式にはウェディングドレスとタキシードを着ます。
We will wear a wedding dress and a tuxedo at our wedding.

02 お色直しには、着物を着るつもりです。
We will change into Japanese *kimono* during the reception.

13 人と付き合う　065

03 披露宴には、100人ほどを招待する予定です。
We plan to invite about 100 people to our wedding reception.

---

04 結婚式は明治神宮で伝統的な日本式にするつもりです。
We plan to have a traditional Japanese-style wedding at Meiji Shrine.

---

05 僕たちは来月、成城の教会で結婚します。
We will exchange marriage vows at a church in Seijo next month.

---

06 結婚のお祝いのお返しは、昔は倍返ししていたそうです。
I heard that people used to give return gifts worth twice as much as what they received from a guest at their wedding.

---

07 現在は半返しで大丈夫です。
Nowadays, you can send return gifts worth half as much as what you have received.

6. 結婚後の展望を語る

01 少なくともしばらくは彼の両親と別居します。
We won't live with his parents, at least not for a while.

---

02 私の両親と同居します。
We will live with my parents.

03 私の両親と二世帯住宅に住むことになっています。
We will live in a two-family house with my parents.

---

04 育メンやる気は十分あります。
I'm going to be a so-called "*ikumen*," or a good father who helps raise his kids.

---

05 育メンなんてやる自信はありません。
I'm not sure if I can be a good partner in raising our kids.

---

06 育メンになれるのなんて暇な人だけ。
Only a man who has plenty of time on his hands can be a so-called *ikumen*.

---

07 一家を支えるためあくせく働くだけしかできません。
The only thing I can do for my family is to work hard to support them.

---

08 結婚しても仕事は続けたいです。
I want to keep working after I get married.

> Note:「結婚しても仕事を続けてもらいたいです」I want my partner to keep pursuing her [his] career after marriage.

---

09 結婚したら専業主婦として、子育てに専念したいです。
I want to stay home after I get married to do a good job raising our children.

13　人と付き合う　　067

10 本音を言えば、嫁さんには外で働くよりは、家にいてぼくに養わしてもらいたいです。

To be honest, I would prefer my wife stay home and let me provide for her rather than work outside.

両親にあいさつする

A： 私と結婚したいなら、両親にきちんと挨拶してほしいの。

If you want to marry me, I want you to meet my parents and ask for their blessing.

両親が賛成してくれなかったら結婚できないわ。

I can't marry you without my parents' blessing.

3 weeks later...

B： お嬢さんとの結婚を許してください。

We want to get married. Will you give us your blessing?

お嬢さんを必ず幸せにします。

I promise I will make your daughter happy.

7. 離婚する

01 離婚しました。
We got divorced. / I'm divorced.

02 事実上、我々は別居中だ。
Effectively, we are separated.

03 家庭内別居をしています。
We still live in the same house, but we live separate lives.

04 相手は外国籍なので、離婚には家庭裁判所に行かないとなりません。

My partner is a foreigner. So to get a divorce, we must go to family court.

---

05 国際結婚なので、離婚するには、家庭裁判所で調停を受けます。

We must go through a mediation process in family court to get divorced, since we are of different nationalities.

---

06 子どもの親権について決めなくてはなりません。

We must agree on which parent is to take custody of our child.

---

07 子どもはまだ幼いので、母親といる方が良いでしょう。

Our child is still very young, so I believe it would be better for the mother to keep the child.

---

08 父親である僕には、子どもと定期的に会う権利があります。

I have the right to see our child regularly as the father.

---

09 財産分与に関しては、弁護士と相談します。

We'll consult with lawyers about the division of property.

---

10 離婚後は夫が家を出て、私と子どもが、この家に住めるようにしてください。

I'd like to ask my husband to move out of this house and let me stay here with our child after our divorce.

11 離婚の原因は、性格の不一致です。
We got a divorce on grounds of incompatibility.

---

12 離婚の原因は、相手の不倫でした。
We got a divorce because he [she] cheated on me [had an affair].

---

13 私たちの離婚の原因は夫による家庭内暴力でした。
We got divorced because of my partner's domestic violence.

> Note：「精神的虐待で」because of mental abuse ／「身体的虐待が原因で」because of physical abuse ／「不当な取り扱いで」because of maltreatment of me.

ハーグ条約

夫［妻］は外国人なので、国際離婚と国境を越えた子の連れ去りについて定めたハーグ条約（「国際的な子の奪取の民事上の側面に関する条約」）の規定をよく知っておく必要があります。

I need to know the provisions of the Hague Abduction Convention [the Hague Convention on the Civil Aspects of International Child Abduction], since my husband [wife] is a foreigner.

離婚をした場合、それまで家族が住んでいた国から勝手に子どもを国外に連れ出すことはできなくなります。

If you get divorced from your husband [wife], you will not be allowed to take your child out of the country you have lived in as a family without the consent of your husband [wife].

No. 14

Chapter 1　Everyday Life

冠婚葬祭

Ceremonies

1. 結婚式に出席する

01 友人の結婚式に招待されたけど、何を着たらいいのか分からない。

I've been invited to my friend's wedding, but I have no idea what to wear for the occasion.

---

02 友達の結婚式なら、ダークグレーとかチャコールとかの暗めのスーツで良いんじゃないかな。

I guess you could go to your friend's wedding in a dark suit, like dark grey or charcoal.

---

03 いとこの結婚披露宴でスピーチを頼まれました。

I have been asked to give a speech at my cousin's wedding reception.

---

04 姪っ子の結婚式には、留袖で行きます。

I'm going to attend my niece's wedding in a black *tomesode kimono*.

Note :「留袖」a black formal *kimono* with richly patterned skirts in front, worn by a married woman（既婚者が着る、裾にたくさん模様の入った黒のフォーマルな着物）。

---

05 会社の同僚の結婚式と披露宴に招かれました。

I've been invited to my colleague's wedding ceremony and the reception.

06 同僚たちからお祝いを集めないと。

I and the other colleagues have to pitch in to give them a gift.

---

07 二次会にも出ようと思っています。

I'm attending the after party.

---

08 二次会っていうのは披露宴のあとに新郎新婦の親しい友人が集まるパーティのことです。

The after party is held for close friends of the couple after the main formal reception.

お祝儀を贈る

ふさわしい祝儀袋を用意しなくては。

We should get an appropriate envelope for the gift.

日本では必ず現金を結婚祝いに贈りますが、アメリカ等では必ずしも現金を贈るわけではありません。

In Japan, we have the custom of always giving cash to marrying couples, but in other countries, such as in the United States, they do not always give cash as a wedding present.

Note：「お祝儀袋」envelope for the gift.「ギフト用の封筒」といえば、現金を包む封筒だと伝わる。

2. 葬儀に参列する

01 今夜おじの通夜［葬儀］に出席します。
I am attending my uncle's wake [funeral] tonight.

02 今夜は、おばの通夜に行ってきます。
I'm going to my aunt's wake.

03 叔母の葬儀では、受付をします。
I'll be acting as a receptionist at my aunt's funeral.

04 私が喪主［施主］を務めます。
I will be acting [serving] as the host at the funeral.

05 正式な喪服を着ないといけません。
I must wear formal mourning attire.

06 お父様のご霊前に献花をさせていただきたいと思います。
We would like to offer flowers with our prayers to the spirit of your father.

07 家族はこぢんまりした穏やかな雰囲気で、父を見送ることができました。
We were very happy we family members could see our father off in a quiet and calm atmosphere.

08 上司に 3 日間の忌引きを願い出ました。
I asked my boss for three days' bereavement leave.

09 会社の帰りに取引先の社長の告別式に参列しますが、平服でといわれています。

I'm attending the funeral of our client's president after work, but I've been told that I should come in an ordinary business suit.

Note :「平服で＝喪服でなくてもよい」I don't need to wear black. としても。

葬儀に関する習慣

■葬儀の際のことば

この度は誠にご愁傷さまです。

Please accept my deepest condolences.

心からお悔やみ申し上げます。

My [Our] deepest condolences to you [to the family of the deceased].

■葬儀の習慣

日本では葬式には香典を持って行きます。

We have the custom of expressing our sorrow and condolences by offering a certain amount of cash in a special envelope at funerals.

不祝儀袋はコンビニで買えます。

We can get a special envelope for a condolence gift at a convenient store.

友人や親せきからの香典返しは、半返しが一般的です。

You should give back a gift that is worth half the amount of the condolence money given by a friend or relative.

お清めの塩をいただきました。家に入る前に、玄関先で使います。

I've got a packet of salt for purification. We powder ourselves with the salt for the ceremonial purification before we step inside the house.

葬儀の告知

先日他界いたしました弊社社長の葬儀を、8月4日ABCメモリアルホールにて執り行います。

We will hold a funeral for our president who recently passed away. The ceremony will be held on August 4th at the ABC Memorial Hall.

土曜日に通夜、日曜日に告別式を挙行いたします。

We will hold a wake on Saturday and the funeral on Sunday.

ご参列いただけると幸いでございます。

We would be very happy if you could join us at the ceremony.

なお、御平服でのご参列をお願い申し上げます。

Please be reminded that black attire is not needed.

家族葬にいたします。御香典、献花はご遠慮申し上げます。

We are seeing our father off in a private ceremony. We cordially request your prayers in lieu of gifts or flowers.

No. 15　　　　　　　　　　　　　　　　Chapter 1　Everyday Life

行事やイベントを楽しむ
Various events

1. 正月

01 年が明けたらその瞬間に友達に携帯[スマホ]で「おめでとう」メールを打ちます。

We text "Happy New Year" to our friends at midnight on New Year's Eve.

Note：text で「携帯で（携帯に）メールを打つ」。

---

02 元旦は、近くの神社に初もうでに行きます。

On New Year's Day, we go to a local shrine to pray for good luck in the coming year.

---

03 お賽銭は、いつもは 100 円以下だけど、この日はちょっと弾みます。

Usually, I put less than 100 yen into the shrine's donation box, but on this day, I'm more generous.

---

04 正月は家族がおばあちゃんのところに集まります。

Our family gets together at our grandma's place on New Year's Day.

---

05 元旦は、祖父母のところに新年のあいさつに行きます。

We visit our grandparents to wish them a Happy New Year.

06 花屋さんに、お正月の生け花に使う松竹梅を買いに行きます。
I'm going to a flower shop to buy pine, bamboo and plum branches for a New Year's flower arrangement.

---

07 書き初めをします。
I do the first calligraphy of the year.

---

08 初夢は良い夢を見たいですね。
We want to have a good first-of-the-year dream on New Year's Day.

---

09 いろはがるたをします。
We play a game with Japanese syllabary cards.

---

10 寝正月ですね。
I just sleep in and relax at home during the New Year's holiday.

---

11 正月休みは、ゆっくりとテレビでスポーツを観戦します。
I enjoy watching sports on TV during the New Year's holiday.

---

12 日本の正月休みは暮れから3日か5日まで1週間くらいあります。
We have about a week-long New Year's holiday in Japan from the end of the previous year to the 3rd or 5th of the new year.

おせち・お雑煮

01 おせちとは、事前に準備して新年の三が日に食べる伝統的な和食で、様々な種類の決まった食材で作られます。

Osechi-dishes are traditional Japanese food prepared in advance for consumption during the first three days of the New Year. They are made up of various specified ingredients.

---

02 おせち料理は数種類しか作りません。

I only prepare a few *osechi*.

---

03 最近の子どもたちは、あまりおせち料理を食べません。

Children nowadays don't eat *osechi*-dishes very much.

---

04 最近は、デパートで豪華なおせち料理も買えます。

Nowadays, we can buy gorgeous, ready-made *osechi*-dishes at department stores.

---

05 お雑煮をいただきます。

We eat *zoni*; soup containing *mochi* [rice cakes], vegetables and other ingredients, popular at the New Year.

福袋

01 ショッピングセンターにお買得の福袋を買いに行きます。

I go to a shopping center to buy a lucky bag, which is a mystery bag filled with items usually worth more than the price of the bag.

02 福袋の中身は普通は見えません。
Usually, we can't see what's inside lucky bags.

03 最近は、中身の一部が見える物（のぞき窓付き）も売っています。
Recently, we find some lucky bags with a peek-in window so that you can see inside a bit.

04 福袋は何が出てくるかわからないところが楽しみでいいのです。
I like buying lucky bags because they give you surprises.

お年玉

01 我々大人は、子どもたちにお年玉をあげます。
We grown-ups give children *otoshidama* [New Year's money], a pretty, little paper envelope with money inside.

02 最近は、両親他、おじさんやおばさんから合わせて数万円もお年玉をもらう子がいるようです。
I understand some children get tens of thousands of yen in *otoshidama* [New Year's money] in total from their parents, uncles and aunts.

03 親せきの子どもたちがたくさんいるので、お年玉が大変です。
I have many little nieces and nephews to give New Year's Day money to. I would have to spend a small fortune.

2. バレンタインデー

01 バレンタインデーには、会社の男性にチョコレートをあげます。
I give chocolate to my male co-workers on Valentine's Day.

02 いつ始まった習慣か知りませんが、日ごろの感謝のしるしです。
I don't know when this custom started, but we do this to express our appreciation to male co-workers.

03 普通は私たち女子社員がお金を集めて合同でチョコを買い、男子社員全員にプレゼントします。
Usually, we girls in the office chip in and buy some chocolate gifts together and give them to all the male workers in office.

04 彼氏［好きな人］には、特別のチョコレートのプレゼントを用意します。
I buy a special chocolate gift for my boyfriend [for the person I have special feelings for].

05 彼氏には自分でチョコのプレゼントをつくるつもりです。
I'm going to make a chocolate gift myself for my boyfriend.

06 バレンタイン・チョコは色々あって、どれを買おうか迷ってしまいます。
I find it difficult to decide on which chocolate to buy on Valentine's Day because there are so many different kinds nowadays.

07 同僚へのチョコは形だけですが、あげないとひどくがっかりされそうです。

I know it's just a token, but if we didn't give one to our co-workers, they would be terribly disappointed.

---

08 お返しを考えるのが面倒なのでチョコはもらいたくないです。

I don't want to be bothered to think what to give in return for the chocolate gifts on Valentine's Day.

義理チョコを渡す

A： 太田さん、私たちから手作りのチョコです。
Mr. Ohta, we've got homemade chocolate for you.

B： えー、本当？！うれしいなあ。
Wow! Really? I'm flattered!

A： ホワイトデーには、豪華なお返し期待してます。
We look forward to something gorgeous in return on White Day!

B： おっと、高くつきそうな義理チョコだなあ。
Uh-oh! Just a token chocolate is going to cost me a lot!

3. ホワイトデー

01 ホワイトデーというのは、日本の菓子メーカーの創作のようです。
I believe White Day is a creation of Japanese candy makers.

02 ホワイトデーはバレンタインデーのひと月後の3月14日です。
White Day comes on March 14th, a month after Valentine's Day.

03 ホワイトデーは、男性から女性にお返しをする日です。
White Day is the day on which men must give back gifts to women.

04 たいていはチョコを返します。
We men usually buy chocolate and give it to girls.

05 職場では私たち男性社員がひと月前のチョコのお返しに女性社員にチョコをあげます。
We guys give chocolate back to female co-workers in return for their chocolate gifts a month before.

4. ひな祭り

01 3月3日はひな祭りを祝います。
We celebrate the *Hina* Doll Festival on March 3rd.

02 ひな祭りには、娘たちの幸せと成長を祈ります。
We pray for our daughters' growth and happiness during the *Hina* Doll Festival.

03 3月3日は祭日ではありません。
March 3rd is not a national holiday.

04 ひな祭りには、昔の宮廷の様子を模した雛人形を飾ります。
We display a *hina* doll set depicting the ancient imperial court.

05 私たちは娘のために、お内裏様に、三人官女、五人囃子を含む7段飾りの雛人形を買いました。
We bought a 7-tiered *hina* doll set, which includes the Emperor and Empress, three court ladies and five court musicians for our daughter.

06 私たちは娘の初節句を祝いました。
We celebrated our daughter's very first *Hina* Doll Festival.

07 この日は、ひなあられや菱餅をいただきます。
On this day, we eat *hina arare*, rainbow-colored puffed rice; and *hishi mochi*, colorful diamond-shaped rice cake.

5. 子どもの日

01 5月5日は祭日で、子どもの日をお祝いします。
We celebrate Children's Day on May 5th, which is a national holiday.

02 5月5日は、昔は男の子の成長を祝う日でした。
We used to observe the day as Boy's Day.

03 男の子の成長を感謝し願ったのです。
We thanked and prayed for boys' healthy growth.

---

04 今もおもちゃの兜や刀を飾る習慣があります。
We still have a custom of exhibiting an artificial *samurai* warriors' helmet and a toy sword.

---

05 ちまきを食べます。
We eat a traditional sweet called *chimaki*; made of sticky cooked rice with herbs and sweet beans inside.

---

06 この日は菖蒲湯に入ります。
We take a bath with iris leaves thrown in the water.

> Note：冬至に入る「ゆず湯」は a *yuzu* bath; a bath in which *yuzu* have been placed.

---

6. ゴールデン・ウィーク（5月の大型連休）

01 4月の終わりから5月のはじめにかけて、大きな連休があります。
We have an early summer holiday week dubbed as "Golden Week" from the end of April through the first week of May.

---

02 連休を利用して多くの人が旅行やレジャーを楽しみます。
Many of us enjoy a trip somewhere or recreational activities over the holiday week.

03 ゴールデン・ウィーク中、行楽地はどこも混雑します。
No matter which resort you go, you will find it very crowded during Golden Week.

7. 七夕

01 私の故郷、仙台では7月に盛大な七夕祭りを行います。
We celebrate a big-scale *Tanabata* or Star Festival in my hometown, Sendai, in July.

02 （七夕には）巨大な吹き流しなど様々な七夕飾りを作ります。
We make all kinds of decorations for the occasion, including gigantic streamers.

03 子どもたちと一緒に、五色の短冊に願い事を書いて大きな竹の枝に吊るします。
We write down our wishes on colorful strips of paper and hang them on a big bamboo branch.

04 私の住んでいる神奈川県平塚市では7月7日ころに七夕祭りがあります。
We celebrate the Star Festival around July 7th in my city of Hiratsuka, Kanagawa Prefecture.

05 子どもたちに、織姫と彦星が天の川を渡って年に一度会うという伝説を語ってきかせます。
We tell our children the legendary story about *Orihime*, the weaver, and her lover, *Hikoboshi*, the cow herder, who are allowed to meet each other by crossing the Milky Way only once a year on this day.

8. 夏休み

01 夏休みには子どもを田舎のおじいちゃん、おばあちゃんのところへ行かせます。

We will send our children to their grandparents', who live in my hometown.

---

02 子どもたちに塾の夏期講習を受けさせます。

We will send our kids to a special summer cram school course.

---

03 夏祭りには花火を楽しみます。

We enjoy fireworks at the summer festival.

---

04 日本の会社では、長い夏休みといっても数日しか取れません。

Many of us working for a Japanese company can only take a few days off for summer vacation.

---

05 同僚に遠慮して、長い夏休みは取りにくいのです。

We hesitate to take a long summer vacation out of consideration for our co-workers.

---

06 最近は、それでも長い休みを取るようになっています。

I think people do take a longer summer vacation nowadays.

---

07 うちの会社では少なくとも1週間の休みを取ってリフレッシュするように言われています。

We are encouraged to take at least a week-long summer vacation in our company.

Note: ⇒ p.97「夏」

9. お盆

01 お盆休みをとって、家族で田舎に帰ります。
I'll take a summer vacation during the *Bon* festival season and visit our parents in the countryside with my family.

02 田舎では先祖の墓参りをします。
We will visit our family grave to pay homage to our ancestors' spirits.

03 お盆には迎え火をたいて、先祖の霊を迎える習慣があります。
We have a custom of making a *Bon* fire to welcome the ancestors' spirits home.

04 灯篭を川へ流します。
We float paper lanterns on the river.

05 毎年恒例の盆踊りが待ち遠しいです。
I'm looking forward to the annual *Bon* dance festival.

10. 敬老の日

01 9月の第3月曜日の敬老の日には祖父母の家に集まります。
We gather together at our grandparents' home on the 3rd Monday of September, which is Respect-for-the-Aged Day.

02 彼ら(祖父母)の長寿を祝い、感謝の意を伝えます。
We celebrate their long, happy lives and express our thanks and love to them.

11. 運動会

01 秋は運動会の季節です。
Autumn is the field day season.

---

02 子どもたちは紅白に分かれて競い合います。
Children are divided into two teams and play against each other.

---

03 今度の日曜は息子の学校の運動会に行きます。
We will go to our son's school athletic meet on Sunday.

Note：「運動会」は Field Day とも。

---

04 5年生の競争に出る息子を応援します。
We will cheer for our son who will run in a fifth graders' race.

---

05 父親パン食い競争に参加しなければなりません。
I have to participate in the father's bun-eat-and-run race.

---

06 日曜日は天気が良くなるよう、てるてる坊主を作ります。
We make a wish for good weather on Sunday by making and hanging good weather charm dolls.

運動会の競技

■徒競走 **footrace**

■二人三脚 **three-legged race**

■クラス対抗リレー **interclass relay race**

- 騎馬戦 a cavalry battle game
- 玉入れ *tamaire*, a game in which balls are thrown into a basket mounted on top of a high pole
- 組み体操 coordinated group gymnastics

12. クリスマス

01 クリスマスイブには、恋人とレストランで食事をします。
I will go out to dinner with my boyfriend [girlfriend] on Christmas Eve.

02 クリスマスには、家にクリスマスケーキを買って帰らないと。
I have to take a Christmas cake home on Christmas Day.

03 クリスマスには子どもが待っていますから、早めに退社します。
I will go home earlier than usual on Christmas Day, as our kids expect me home for dinner.

04 子どもとクリスマスツリーを飾ります。
We decorate a Christmas tree with our children.

05 子どもがサンタにどんなおもちゃを頼んでいるのか聞き出さなくちゃ。
I have to find out what toys our kids are asking for from Santa.

06 まだうちの子はサンタクロースを信じています。
Our children still believe in Santa Claus, you know.

07 子どもが寝るのを待って、プレゼントを枕元に置きます。
I have to make sure our children are fast asleep before I place their gifts at their bedside.

08 子どもに、サンタについて本当の事を言うべきかどうか迷います。
I don't know if I should tell our children the truth about Santa yet.

09 子どもの夢を壊したくないですよね。
I don't want to crush the kids' dream (about Santa Claus).

10 クリスマスには、フライドチキンを買って帰ります。
I will take home fried chicken for Christmas dinner.

11 クリスマスには、雪が降ると良いです。
I would love to have a white Christmas.

13. 大みそか

01 大みそかの0時ごろに友達と神社に行きます。
On New Year's Eve, I go to a shrine around midnight with friends.

そうすると、無事に年を越せたことへの感謝を示すとともに、新しい年の幸せもお祈りできます。
We can both thank for blessings for the past year and ask for continued blessings for the New Year.

02 近くのお寺に行って除夜の鐘をつくのに参加します。

I go to a temple nearby and join the crowd ringing the bell 108 times to shed off all the misfortunes of the past year.

---

03 大みそかには（長寿を願って）年越しそばを食べます。

We eat *soba* noodles on New Year's Eve, praying for a life that is long like *soba* noodles.

---

04 大みそかは、ギリギリまで大掃除で忙しいです。

We will be busy cleaning up our home till the last moment on New Year's Eve.

> Note:「おせち料理を作るのに忙しい」We will be busy cooking traditional Japanese New Year's dishes called *osechi*.
> 「年賀状を書くのに忙しい」I will be busy writing New Year's cards.

---

05 小さな子どもも大みそかだけは夜更かししてテレビを観るのを許されます。

We allow even very young children to stay up late on the last day of the year to watch television.

> Note:「紅白歌合戦」The annual contest between male and female popular singers on New Year's Eve, sponsored and broadcast by NHK（毎年、NHK が大みそかに放送している、人気の歌手が男性と女性に分かれて競う番組）。

14. オリンピック

01 2020年の東京オリンピックがすごく楽しみです。
I'm really looking forward to the 2020 Tokyo Olympic Games.

02 私は体操や陸上競技が楽しみです。
I love to watch gymnastics and track and field events.

03 競歩で有望な日本人選手が出てきました。
We now have a very promising Japanese racewalker.

04 フェンシングは、是非会場に観戦に行きたいです。
I'd like to go to the event venue to observe fencing.

05 野球が競技から漏れたら本当に残念です。
I think it would really be a shame if baseball were eliminated from the Olympics.

06 選手村でボランティアをしようかと思っています。
I'm thinking about doing volunteer work in the Olympic village.

07 国の内外から多くの人がくるでしょう。
I'm sure we will have a large number of visitors both from other parts of Japan and from abroad.

08 お客様をおもてなしの心で迎えたいですね。

I hope to welcome all the visitors with the Japanese spirit of hospitality.

---

09 2020年のオリンピックの前に、2016年にはリオ・オリンピックがあります。

Before the 2020 Olympics, we also have the 2016 Rio Olympics.

---

15. サッカーワールドカップ

01 ロシアで開催される2018年FIFAワールドカップを現地で観戦したいと思っています。

I want to go to the event venue to watch the 2018 FIFA World Cup matches to be held in Russia.

Note:「応援ツアーでロシアに行きます」I'm traveling to Russia on a cheer-the-national-team tour.

---

02 本大会にでるのは32チームです。

Thirty-two teams will be playing in the final tournament.

---

03 ワールドカップ開催国のロシアは予選を免除されます。

Russia, the host country of the FIFA World Cup, is exempted from playing in the qualifiers.

---

04 本大会では緒戦で日本が強いチームとあたらないとよいのですが。

I hope Japan will not need to play against very strong teams in the initial round of the World Cup final.

15　行事やイベントを楽しむ　　093

05 予選は、アジア、アフリカ、北中米カリブ海、南米、オセアニア、ヨーロッパ予選と6地域で行われます。

Qualifiers will be played in six regions: Asia, Africa, North and Central America and the Caribbean, South America, Oceania, and Europe.

---

06 新監督のハリル・ホジッチ監督はどう思いますか。

What do you think of the new manager for the Japanese national team, Vahid Halilhodzic?

---

07 日本にはぜひワールドカップ本大会まで行ってほしいです。

I want Japan to advance to the FIFA World Cup finals.

---

08 日本女子代表のなでしこジャパンの活躍を誇りに思いました。

I felt very proud of the Japanese women's national team, *Nadeshiko* Japan, for their superb performance.

---

09 ヨーロッパの名門チームで活躍する良い選手もたくさん出てきていますよね。

We now have excellent players doing well in prestigious teams in Europe.

---

10 日本のサッカーもよくここまで来ましたよ。

I would say Japan's soccer has come a long way.

No. 16

Chapter 1　Everyday Life

日本の四季について話す
Talking about Japan's four seasons

1. 春

01 春が来ました。
Spring is here. / Spring has come.

02 春らしい陽気ですね。
It is spring weather, isn't it?

03 近所の公園に花見に行きます。
I go to a nearby park to see the cherry blossoms.

04 一緒にイチゴ狩りに行きましょう。
Let's go strawberry picking.

05 一年で最初に吹く強い南風は、春がくる前ぶれです。
The first strong south winds of the year signal the arrival of spring.

> Note：春一番 the first spring gale.

2. 花粉症

01 花粉の季節が始まりました。

The pollen season has set in.

Note：花粉症 pollinosis.

---

02 今日は花粉がたくさん飛んでいます。

There's a lot of pollen in the air today.

---

03 毎年、春は花粉症に苦しみます。

I suffer from hay fever every spring.

---

04 花粉が目のかゆみと鼻水とくしゃみを引き起こします。

Pollen makes my eyes feel itchy, my nose run and me sneeze.

Note：スギ花粉 cedar pollen ／ブタクサ花粉 ragweed pollen.

---

3. 梅雨

01 梅雨入りしました。

The rainy season has set in.

---

02 梅雨明けしました。

The rainy season is over.

---

03 梅雨は冷えます。

We have a cold spell during the rainy season.

4. 夏

01 蒸し暑いです。
It's terribly hot and humid.

02 日増しに暑くなります。
It's getting hotter day by day.

03 東京の夏はすごく暑いです。
The summer is very hot in Tokyo.

04 9月に入り、夏は終わりましたが、残暑が厳しいです。
Summer was over in September, but we are still experiencing the heat of summer.

05 北海道へ避暑に行きました。
I went to Hokkaido for the summer.

06 高校野球観戦が楽しみです。
I look forward to watching the annual high school baseball games.

07 熱中症にかからないように注意が必要です。
You must be careful not to suffer from heatstroke.

08 小まめに水分補給をしなければなりません。
You must make sure you drink enough liquid.

09 エアコンも上手に使わなくてはなりません。
You must also use the air-conditioner when needed.

> **土用の丑の日**
>
> 土用の丑の日にはうなぎを食べてエネルギーを補給する習慣があります。
>
> We have a custom of getting extra energy by eating *unagi*, barbecued eel, on Midsummer Day of the Ox, which falls on a different day every year, but always between near the end of July and the beginning of August.

5. 秋

01 読書の秋です。
Autumn is the best season for reading.

---

02 秋は気候がいいです。
The weather in autumn is good.

---

03 栗、松茸、そして秋刀魚といった秋の味覚を楽しみました。
We really enjoyed the autumn food, like Japanese chestnuts, *matsutake* mushrooms, and Pacific sauries.

---

04 毎年、高尾山に紅葉狩りに行きます。
I go to Mt. Takao to enjoy the autumn colors every year.

6. 冬

01 今年は暖冬です。
It's a mild [warm] winter this year.

Note:「寒い冬」は a severe [hard, cold] winter.

---

02 沖縄に避寒して数日過ごしました。
I escaped winter for several days in Okinawa.

---

03 冬は空気が非常に乾燥します。
The air is extremely dry in winter.

---

04 毎年冬になると手があかぎれになります。
Every winter I get chapped hands.

---

05 風邪[インフルエンザ]が流行っています。
A cold [The flu] is going around.

---

06 冬になると風邪をよくひきます。
I often catch cold in winter.

---

07 風邪予防のため、家に帰ると手洗いうがいをしています。
Every time I come home, I wash my hands and gargle to prevent a cold.

Note:⇒ p. 190「スキー・スノーボードをする」

Chapter 2

働く
Work

多くの人にとって
1日の大半の時間を占める
「仕事」について、
英語で語ってみましょう。

No. 01

Chapter 2　Work

仕事を志望する

Choosing a job

01 できれば良いところに就職して生涯そこで働きたいです。
If I can, I want a job in a good company where I can work for my entire career.

02 公務員は安定していていいと思います。
I think a job as a public servant would be nice, since it would be a stable one.

03 国家公務員の上級試験を受けるつもりです。
I'm going to take the advanced civil service examination.

04 金融機関に勤めたいと思っています。
I hope to find a job with a financial institution.

05 ジャーナリストになりたいので新聞社の試験を受けます。
I want to be a journalist, so I will be applying for a job [a position] in the newspaper business.

06 メーカーに勤めたいです。
I want to work for a manufacturer.

07 研究開発の仕事がしたいです。
I wish to work in the R&D section [department].

08 IT企業に勤めたいです。
I would like to work for an IT company.

09 商社でバイヤーをやりたいです。
I would like to work as a buyer at a trading company.

10 英語を使える仕事がしたいです。
I would like a job which requires the use of English.

11 手に職をつけたいです。
I would like to acquire professional skills.

12 会計士とか看護師とかの資格を取りたいです。
I want to obtain certification to become an accountant or a nurse.

13 起業したいです。
I want to start my own company.

14 専門職に就きたいです。
I would like a job as a professional.

15 私の夢は音楽で身を立てることです。
My dream is to make a living with music.

16 子どもが小さいので、10：00〜3：00位のパートタイムで働きたいです。
Our kids are still very young, so I want to work part-time, something like 10:00 to 3:00.

No. 02

Chapter 2　Work

就職活動をする

Looking for a job

1. 就職活動をする

01 就活中です。
I'm looking [hunting] for a job now.

02 総合職につくつもりです。
I'm looking for a management-track position.

03 一般職を探しています。
I'm looking for regular office work.

04 フルタイムの仕事に就きたいです。
I want a full-time position [job].

05 アルバイトを探しています。
I'm looking for a part-time job.

06 もう20件くらいの就職試験を受けましたが、まだ内定をもらえていません。
I've sat for about 20 company exams, but I haven't got any job offers yet.

07 午後に面接があります。
I have an interview this afternoon.

08 三石商事から内定をもらいました。
I got an offer from Mitsuishi Corporation.

売り手市場・買い手市場

今年の就職は売り手市場です。
This year the labor market has become a sellers' market.

買い手市場です。
We are in a buyers' market.

---

2. 就職のための勉強をする

01 プロのウェブ・デザイナーになるためいくつかウェブ・デザイン・トレーニング・コースを取っています。
I'm taking some web design training courses to become a professional web designer.

02 司法試験に来年再挑戦します。
I will be taking the bar exam for the second time next year.

03 来年、公認会計士試験を受けます。
I will take the certified public accountant [CPA] examination next year.

04 社会福祉士になりたいです。
I want to be a certified social worker.

05 学生のうちに教員資格を取りたいと思います。
I want to acquire a teacher's qualification before I graduate.

06 航空会社のパイロットになりたいです。

I want to be an airline pilot.

---

07 航空会社のパイロットになるには、1500時間以上の飛行経験が必要です。

To qualify as an airline pilot, you must have more than 1500 hours of flight experience.

---

08 しっかりしたコミュニケーション能力、問題解決力と観察能力がないとパイロットにはなれません。

I need to have strong communication, problem-solving and observation skills to start a career as a pilot.

No. 03

Chapter 2 Work

自分の仕事について話す
Talking about your job

01 中小企業［大企業］で働いています。
I work for a small company [a big company].

02 外資系企業で働いています。
I work for a foreign affiliated company.

03 自営業です。
I work for myself.

04 会社を経営しています。
I own a company.

05 会社の役員（取締役）です。
I am on my company's board.

1. 事務職

01 営業事務の仕事をしています。
I am an office clerk in the sales department.

02 営業担当者のサポートがおもな仕事です。
I provide support to the sales staff mostly.

03 書類にミスがないか、ダブルチェックをするようにしています。
I always make sure to double-check the contents of papers so I make no mistakes.

---

04 ワードやエクセルで書類を作成するほか、パワーポイントを使ってプレゼンテーションの資料を作ることもあります。
I use Word and Excel to create documents, and sometimes use Power Point to prepare presentation materials.

---

05 秘書の仕事につきました。
I got a secretarial job.

---

06 英文の手紙や書類を日本語に翻訳する仕事をしています。
I am a translator. I translate letters and documents from English into Japanese.

---

07 新商品企画の社内コンペに応募しました。
I entered an in-house competition for new product development.

お茶くみ

A: 田中さん、お茶は自分で入れるから。君はお茶くみはしなくていいよ。
Ms. Tanaka, I can make tea for myself. You don't need to make tea for me, or for anyone else for that matter.

この会社じゃ、お茶は自分で入れるのがルールだから。
In our office, we all make our tea ourselves. That is the rule in this office.

... 10 minutes later

B: お客さんが4名お見えになり、佐藤部長と私とで応対しますので、会議室にお茶を6個お願いできますか？

We have 4 visitors with us. Mr. Sato and I will meet with them in the meeting room. Will you make six cups of tea for us?

2. 経理

01 経理の仕事をしています。
I work in the accounting department.

02 決算の時期には毎日残業です。
I have to work overtime everyday during the weeks up to the end of the account settlement period.

03 関係部署に経費削減の提案を行いました。
I recommended [proposed] that the relevant departments cut costs.

3. 公務員

01 市役所で働いています。
I work for the city government.

02 選挙の時期には大変な業務量です。
We have so much work to do when there are elections.

03 終電帰りが当たり前です。
Usually, we have to work till so late at night that we get used to taking the last train home.

---

04 窓口業務では市民から厳しい意見をもらうこともあります。
We sometimes get criticized pretty badly by citizens who come to use our services at the city office.

---

4. コールセンターで働く

01 コールセンターで働いています。
I work in the call center.

---

02 顧客からのクレームがあった場合には、まず相手の言ったことを確認して、非があった部分について謝ります。
When we get a complaint from a customer, we first check if the claim is valid, and if it is, we offer an apology for whatever we've done wrong.

---

03 その後、対応について検討し、しかるべき部署に対応してもらいます。
We will then study how we should handle the matter [complaint], and have the appropriate department take care of the case.

5. シフト勤務

01 シフト勤務の職場で働いています。
I work on a shift system.

02 できれば夜のシフトは避けたいです。
If possible, I would rather not work a night shift.

6. エンジニア

01 プロジェクトのリーダーを任されました。
I am the leader of the project.

02 顧客の職場に出向してシステム開発を行っています。
I am loaned to one of our customers to engage in system development.

03 社内SEとして、会社内のシステムの管理をしています。
I am an in-house system engineer. I manage computer systems in the company.

04 現場で最先端技術の指導を受けています。
I'm taking on-the-job lessons on the state-of-the-art technology.

05 工作機械の操作について直接現場で指導を受けています。
I'm given hands-on training on the operation of various machine tools.

06 虚弱なお年寄りを支援するためのロボット制作チームの一員です。
I'm a member of the team that manufactures robots to help the frail elderly.

---

07 障害のある人を助けるための人型ロボットの開発に携わっています。
I'm involved in the development of humanoids to help people with physical disabilities.

7. 営業の仕事

01 毎月の営業ノルマがあります。
Each one of us has a monthly target or quota to meet in our sales operations.

---

02 未達成の場合、みんなの前で叱責されます。
If I fail to meet it, I get admonished in front of my colleagues.

---

03 未達成の場合、上司と面談して翌月の改善案を提出します。
If I fail to meet it, I get interviewed by my boss and I'm required to offer him [her] my plans on how I intend to do better the following month.

---

04 到底、達成できないノルマが課せられています。
We are given a vastly unachievable quota to meet.

---

05 飛び込み営業をしています。
I make rounds to potential customers' offices to sell our products.

06 ルート営業（すでに取引のある顧客を定期的に訪問する）なのでノルマはありません。

I just have a number of fixed customers to visit regularly to sell our products without any set sales target.

---

07 自社製品を自分で買って販売ノルマを達成する会社もあると聞きます。

I hear some sales workers make purchases of some of their own company's products to meet their sales target [quota].

8. 教育にかかわる仕事

01 保育士をしています。

I am a certified nursery school teacher.

---

02 毎日、子どもたちの様子を父母への連絡帳に記録します。

I keep a journal for each child to let the parents know how their child was during the day.

---

03 子どもたちはみな素直でかわいいです。

I like each and every one of the children. They are all adorable.

---

04 父母参観、運動会、誕生会など行事に追われています。

We are always busy with a variety of events of the school, such as Parents' Day, Sport's Day and kids' birthday parties.

05 小学校の教師をしています。
I am an elementary school teacher.

---

06 小学校教師なので、担当クラスのほとんど全ての科目を教えています。
As an elementary school teacher, I teach almost all the subjects to my class.

---

07 今年は1年生の担任になりました。
I am in charge of a class of first graders this year.

---

08 中学校で数学の教師をしています。
I am a junior high math teacher.

---

09 担任の仕事とテニス部の顧問とで大忙しです。
I am very busy as I am a homeroom teacher and also a coach of a students' tennis club.

---

10 家に生徒の答案を持ち帰ってテストの採点をしています。
I take students' exam papers home to mark them.

---

11 大学で非常勤講師をしています。
I teach part-time at a university.

---

12 京葉大学と赤坂大学で初級ラテン語を週に2コマずつ教えています。
I teach 2 classes each of first year Latin at Keiyo and Akasaka Universities every week.

9. 派遣・パートで仕事をする

01 派遣で仕事をしています。
I'm a temp [temporary] worker.

---

02 今の仕事は有期雇用です。常勤フルタイムの仕事が欲しいです。
I'm working for a fixed period. I would like a regular, full-time job.

---

03 正社員と同じ仕事をしていますが賃金は安いです。
I do basically the same work as a regular employee at the company, but get paid less.

---

04 今の派遣の仕事はそろそろ3年になりますから、来年は契約切れでクビになるんじゃないかと思います。
I've been working as a temp worker for the company for almost three years, so I'm afraid they are going to fire me when my contract is up.

---

05 常勤になれるよう会社に申し入れます。
I intend to ask the company to hire me as a regular full-time worker.

> Note：4, 5 は派遣社員が同じ職場で3年働いた場合、企業が直接雇用するか契約を更新しないかいずれかになることから。

---

06 フルタイムで働かないかと誘われています。
I got an offer for a full-time position.

No. 04

Chapter 2　Work

職場について話す

Talking about your office

1. 会社について話す

01 弊社では、提案があれば必ず1ページにまとめて会議で発表することが求められます。

When we have a proposal, we all are required to have a one-page document of ideas to present at a conference in our company.

---

02 各自のアイデアをきちんとまとめて、会議でもっとうまく発表できるようにすべきです。

We should be able to organize our ideas better and be able to present them at the meeting more effectively.

---

03 クライアントへのプレゼン会議は、来週火曜日の午後です。

We will give a presentation to the client next Tuesday afternoon.

---

04 セールスのノウハウは、職場の先輩から教えてもらえると思います。

I think I can learn good salesmanship from some of the senior members of the office.

05 先輩のやり方をよく観察して、スキルを盗もうと思っています。

I observe the work of my seniors to steal their skills.

---

06 厳しいですが思いやりのある指導者が職場にいて幸運だと思います。

I feel lucky to have a very demanding but considerate mentor at work.

---

07 今の仕事はすごい長時間勤務なので、新しい仕事を探しています。

I'm looking for a new job because I have to put in so many hours now.

---

08 今の会社はブラック企業ですよ。できるだけ早く辞めたいです。

The company I work for exploits its workers [treats its workers terribly]. I want to quit as soon as possible.

Note：exploit「搾取する、(労働力を) 食い物にする」。「ブラック企業」の語感に近い。

---

09 結婚して姓が変わったのですが、名前を変えるのが面倒なので、旧姓のままで仕事をしています。

I got married and my official surname is different now. But it is too much trouble to go by my partner's name. So I continue to use my maiden name in business.

---

10 せっかく仕事を早く終わらせても、その分、別の仕事を押し付けられます。

I can finish my work quickly, but it doesn't help, because I get more work to do anyhow.

11 ほかの人に迷惑がかかるので、基本的に有給休暇は使えません。
I cannot take my paid holidays basically, because it would cause trouble to others in office.

---

12 全社員が（自動的に）労働組合に加入しています。
All the employees of the company are (automatically) members of the company labor union.

---

2. 上司や同僚について話す

01 職場にようやく慣れて来ました。
I'm getting used to my job.

---

02 うちの課長は、案外細かいことに気がつく人ですよね。
I noticed our section chief pays attention to details.

Note：「細かいことにうるさい人」は a stickler for details.

---

03 課長があまりうるさくない人でよかったですよ。
I'm glad our section chief is easy to please.

---

04 やることさえちゃんとやっておけば、自由にさせてくれます。
We are left rather free to do anything, as long as we do what we should do properly.

---

05 私は部長として、状況によっては厳しくしなければなりません。
As a general manager, I would have to be strict, depending on the situation.

06 新人のOJT教育を任されました。
I am responsible now for the on-the-job training of the newly recruited.

コピーを頼む

A： 高田さん、悪いけど、この書類コピーしてくれます？
Mr. Takada, I'm sorry to bother you, but I want you to make copies of this document.

B： はい、何部コピーしますか。
Certainly! How many sets (would you like)?

A： ウィリアムズくん、この書類コピーして！
Mr. Williams, will you make copies of this document?

B： それは、私の仕事じゃありません。
That is not my job.

A： そうか、文化の違いだなあ。
All right. I guess this is a cultural difference.

---

3. 歓送迎会・社員旅行

01 新人のための歓迎会を計画します。
I'll organize a welcome party for our new staff members.

02 会社からの補助が出ます。
We get some financial help from the company.

03 課長が会費以上に出してくれると思います。
I think our section chief will pay more than his normal share out of his pocket.

04 会費は 5000 円です。
We ask everyone to chip in 5,000 yen per person (to join the party).

---

05 石毛さんに余興係を頼みます。
I'll ask Mr. Ishige to be in charge of the entertainment program.

---

06 上田さんが今度大阪支社に転勤ですよね。送別会をやらないと。
We would like to organize a farewell party for Mr. Ueda, since he is getting transferred to the Osaka Branch.

---

07 太田さんが来月ニューヨークに転勤しますので、皆さん、餞別をお願いします。
I ask everyone to chip in to the farewell fund for Ms. Ohta, who is being transferred to New York next month.

---

08 私の会社は、毎年、社員旅行に行きます。今年の行先は台湾です。
We take a company trip every year. We are going to Taiwan this year.

---

09 今年は、私が社員旅行の幹事を仰せつかりました。
This year, I have the honor of acting as the organizer of the annual company trip.

No. 05

Chapter 2 Work

転職する
Changing jobs

01 転職したいと思っています。
I want to change jobs.

---

02 もうちょっと条件の良い仕事を探しています。
I'm looking for a better job.

Note:「もっと給料の良い仕事に就きたいです」I want a better-paying job.

---

03 最初の仕事はすごく給料が安くて、父から借金しなければなりませんでした。
My first job paid very little, and I had to borrow from my father.

---

04 今の仕事はちょっと面白くなくなってきています。
I've started to feel a bit bored with my current work.

---

05 転職すると言っても、簡単じゃないのはわかっているんですが。
I know it won't be easy to find a better job.

---

06 生涯同じ会社で働くつもりはありません。
I don't intend to work for one [the same] company for my entire career.

07 もう3年働きましたから、何か新しい、別の仕事をしたいです。
I've worked for the company for 3 years, so I want to find a fresh, different job opportunity.

---

08 もっと自分の能力が発揮できる仕事に就きたいです。
I want a job that will allow me to use my abilities more.

---

09 自分の能力開発につながる仕事に移りたいです。
I would like to get a job that will help me develop my skills.

---

10 女性にもガラスの天井がない職場に移りたいです。
I would like to find a new work place where there is no glass ceiling for women.

---

11 同僚と人間関係がうまくいってなくて、転職したいです。
I'm not getting along well with my colleagues at work, so I want to change jobs.

---

12 30歳を過ぎたので、転職先は本当に限られています。
I am over 30 now. So if I want to change jobs, new opportunities are very limited.

---

13 仕事でキャリアを積んでから転職する場合は、職場の即戦力になることが求められます。
If we want to change jobs mid-career, we are expected to start making tangible contributions to the work of the new company immediately.

14 ヘッドハンターに声を掛けられています。
I've gotten calls from some headhunters.

---

15 ヘッドハンターには、その気になったら連絡すると言ってあります。
I've told the headhunters that I will call them when I am serious about changing jobs.

No. 06　　　　　　　　　　　　　　　　　Chapter 2　Work

退職する

Leaving the company

1. 事情があって退職する

01 一身上の都合で退職しました。
I left the company for personal reasons.

> Note:「一身上の都合により退職を願い出ました」I tendered my resignation for personal reasons.

02 結婚するので退職しました。
I left the company because I was going to get married.

03 寿退社はもう古いですよね。
I think it is a thing of the past for a woman to have to quit a company when she gets married.

04 結局、子どもの世話で退職を迫られるのは女性です。
It's always the mother who has to quit work to take care of children.

05 保育園が見つからないので、しばらく仕事を辞めるほかありません。
I must quit working, at least for a while, because we can't find a day care to send our child to.

06 子どもたちに手がかかるので、辞めざるをえません。
I have to quit my job because I must take care of our children.

---

07 親の介護で退職しなければなりませんでした。
I had to retire from my job to care for my elderly parents.

---

08 一時退職して、新しいIT技術を身につけるため、学校に行くつもりです。
I'm going to take a break from work and take a training course to learn new ICT skills.

> Note：ICT =information and communication technology「IT技術」。

---

09 早期退職を希望して、退職金で起業しました。
I volunteered to retire early and established my own company with the retirement allowance.

---

10 入社2年目からまともな仕事を与えられず、退職せざるをえませんでした。
I didn't get to do any decent work in the company from the second year on, so I had to quit.

2. 会社が倒産する

01 会社が倒産して失業しました。
I lost my job because the company I was working for went bankrupt.

02 当然、退職金は出ませんでした。
Of course, I didn't get any severance pay from them.

03 収入は失業保険のみになりました。
So I only have unemployment insurance benefits to rely on as income now.

3. 再就職する

01 会社を定年退職しました。
I retired (at the official retirement age).

02 ハローワークや人材会社に通って再就職先を探しています。
I have been looking for a new job opportunity at the public job placement office, Hello Work, and private staffing agencies.

03 退職後に公共の職業訓練学校に通い、介護福祉士の資格を取りました。
After I retired, I took occupational training at a government-operated training institution and obtained a certified care worker's license.

04 老人ホームに就職しました。
I have found a job at a nursing home.

Note：nursing home で「老人ホーム」。

嘱託で働く

60歳で定年退職をしましたが、社内の再雇用制度で65歳まで嘱託で働きます。

I officially retired at age 60, but I will continue to work for the same company till 65 as a part-time commissioned worker, since the company has a rehiring system for their former regular employees.

No. 07

Chapter 2　Work

労働条件・福利厚生を調べる
Labor conditions

1. 賃金について聞く

Q 時給はいくらですか。
What's the hourly wage?

時給 1000 円です。
The hourly wage is 1,000 yen.

Q 初任給はいくらですか。
What is the starting salary?

大卒で月 250,000 円です。
We pay 250,000 yen per month to a college graduate.

高卒の初任給は 150,000 円です。
We pay 150,000 yen a month to a high school graduate.

Note:「手取りはいくらですか？」How much do I get to take home a month?

Q ボーナスはありますか。
Do you pay a bonus? /Do I get a bonus?

ボーナスは当然会社の業績次第ですが、最初は年に月給4カ月分程度です。
It depends, of course, on the company's performance, but we usually pay a bonus worth 4 months' pay a year to a starting worker.

Q 時間外労働はどうなっていますか。
What is your overtime policy?

通常の時給の1.2倍を払います。
We pay 1.2 times your usual hourly wage.

2. 労働時間について聞く

Q 労働時間はどうなっていますか。
What are your working hours like?

労働時間は午前午後の15分ずつの休憩と昼休み45分を含めて1日9時間15分です。
We want you to put in 9 hours and 15 minutes a day, including two 15-minute breaks, one in the morning and one in the afternoon, as well as a 45-minute lunch break.

Q 土日は毎週休みですか。
Will I have weekends off?

土日は例外を除いて、完全に全社員が休みです。
We have all our employees take weekends off, except for some exceptional occasions.

週休2日制ですが、土日に関しては交代で休暇を取ってもらいます。
We give you 2 days off a week. But we ask our employees to take turns taking weekends off.

3. 福利厚生について聞く

Q 福利厚生はどうなっていますか。
What kind of benefits do you have for your employees?

01 有給休暇は年に20日です。
We give 20 paid holidays a year.

02 有給はできるだけ毎年消化してほしいと思います。
We want our employees take all the paid holidays every year.

03 育児休暇は男女とも1年です。
We give a year-long child care leave both to female and male employees.

04 家賃補助があります。
We give a rent subsidy.

05 会社の寮もあります。
We also have a dormitory [apartments] for employees.

---

06 営業の仕事の場合は、営業手当があります。
If you work in the sales department, we also give you a sales person's allowance.

---

07 家族がいる場合は、扶養手当があります。
If you have a family, we pay a family allowance.

---

08 休暇に利用できる施設も4か所にあります。
We have 4 hotels [facilities] available for employees and their families' holiday use.

---

09 失業保険制度に入っています。
We subscribe to the unemployment insurance system.

---

10 本社の近くに社内保育園も用意しています。
We have an in-house day care for our employees' young children near the headquarters.

---

11 フレックスタイム制度があり、子育て中の社員は男性も女性も利用できます。
We have a flexible working system which can be utilized by both male and female employees raising a family.

12 子育て中は 1 日 4-5 時間の短時間労働もできます。
You can work short days, 4 to 5 hours a day, while you are raising young children.

13 子どもが小さいうちは、在宅勤務もできます。
You can also telecommute from home while your children are very young.

Q 厚生年金と健康保険制度がありますか。
Are employees enrolled in the Employee Pension and Health Insurance Programs?

01 厚生年金に加入しています。
Employees are enrolled in the Employee Pension program.

02 厚生年金制度には入っていないので、国民年金に入ってもらうことになります。
Employees are not enrolled in the Employee Pension program, so you would have to join the National Pension program yourself.

03 健康保険に加入しています。
Employees are enrolled in the Employee Health Insurance program.

04 健康保険制度はありませんから、国民健康保険に入って下さい。
Employees are not enrolled in the Employee Health Insurance program, so you are advised to join your local National Health Insurance program yourself.

05 労災保険により勤務中に事故にあわれた場合には保険金が支払われます。

Industrial accident insurance [Workmen's Compensation (Insurance)] will cover you if you have an accident at work.

4. 過労死の問題

01 我々日本人は働き過ぎですね。過労死なんてケースもあります。

I think many of us Japanese are working too many hours. We even see cases of workers dying from overwork sometimes.

02 若くして過労死なんてことにならないよう、働き方に気をつけないと。

We'd better be careful about the way we work to avoid a premature death from overwork.

03 毎日仕事のストレスが多くて、気が狂いそうなんです。

I've got so much stress at work every day that I'm going crazy.

04 過労死しちゃいそう。

I could die from overwork.

No. 08

Chapter 2 Work

昇給する

Getting a pay raise

01 そろそろ昇給があってもいい頃です。
It's about time we get a pay raise.

02 基本給の賃上げでは、なかなか会社を説得できません。
We can't easily persuade our employer to give us a basic wage hike.

03 景気の改善で、ようやく給料が上がりそうです。
We will probably get a pay raise finally, as the economy has been improving.

04 会社の業績が良くなっているんですから、給料が上がるよう、今年の春闘では組合には頑張ってほしいです。
Our company's performance has been improving, so we want the union to do well in this year's spring wage negotiations.

05 平均160円の賃上げで労使が合意したそうです。
I hear our company and the union have agreed on a 160-yen wage hike on the average.

06 我々女性は男性と比べて昇給率が低いのは非常に不当だと思っています。

We female employees feel it's really unfair that we get much smaller wage hikes than those given to the male workers.

---

07 先月の営業成績が良かったので、特別ボーナスがありました。

We had a pretty good sales performance last month, so we got a special bonus.

No. 09

Chapter 2 Work

出世する

Getting promoted

01 課長に昇格しました。
I got promoted to section chief.

02 外資系企業では、転職する度に出世するのが普通だそうですよ。
I hear it's normal that you get a higher position in a new company every time you change jobs in the world of foreign firms.

03 出世はやっぱり嬉しいですよね。
I would be happy, of course, if I got promoted. Anybody would be happy, I'm sure.

04 私はあんまり社会的なスキルがなくて、なかなか出世しないんですよ。
I have pretty poor social skills, so I don't get promoted easily.

05 出世のためには、ある程度社交のスキルがないと。
You have to have some good social skills if you want to be promoted in a company.

06 出世の武器は能力と成績ばかりじゃないってことに気づきました。

I've realized that there are other important tools needed to get promoted besides just your competence and achievements.

---

07 出世するにはやはり能力と成績が基本ですよ。

I believe basically you get promoted on the basis of your competence and achievements.

---

08 仕事で出世するばかりが人生の目的じゃありませんよね。

I don't think the final objective of a person's life is to be a successful businessperson.

---

09 出世コースに乗っているとは言えないです。

I can't say I'm on a fast promotion track.

総合職と一般職

女性には出世の見込みのある総合職と、そうでない一般職というくくりがあるなんて日本ぐらいでしょう。

I would say it's only in Japan that we have career and non-career tracks for female workers to divide them into ones who have the prospect of promotion and ones who do not to start with.

No. 10

Chapter 2　Work

通勤する

Commuting

1. 通勤時間

01 会社から歩いて［バスで、電車で］帰ります。
I walk [take a bus / take trains] home from the office.

02 通勤には往復3時間もかかります。
I have to spend three hours commuting to and from our office.

03 家から職場まで1時間程度という人が多いですね。
Many of us spend about one hour getting to work from home.

04 職場まで車で5分なんてうらやましいですね。
I really envy those who only need to drive 5 minutes to the office.

2. 電車で通勤する

01 家から職場に行くのに3回も乗り換えをしなければなりません。
I have to change trains three times to get to work from home.

02 新しい路線が開通したので通勤が便利になりました。
A new train line just opened, so it is much more convenient for me to commute now.

---

03 通勤にも他の外出にも便利な Suica を使っています。
I use a very convenient Suica card, a kind of a train pass, to commute and to go anywhere else.

---

04 Suica は、定期券としても使えるし、東京のだいたいの路線で運賃の支払いに使えます。
We can use a Suica card as a prepaid commuter pass and to pay for other rides on most train lines in Tokyo.

---

05 カードリーダーに IC カードをかざすだけで改札を通れます。
You just need to place your IC card over the card reader at the gate to go through.

---

06 ちゃんとカードをかざさないと、ゲートが開かなくて引っかかっちゃう時があります。
You can get stopped by the gate if you fail to hold your card properly over the reader.

---

07 携帯電話を使って、電車賃も支払っています。
I'm using my mobile phone to pay for train rides, too.

---

08 ラッシュの時間にベビーカーで乗ってくるお母さんがいるといやですね。
I hate to be near a mother with a baby carriage during rush hour.

09 赤ちゃんと移動しなければならない親は大変ですから、助けてあげないと。
We must help parents with babies on trains because it's not easy to travel with them.

---

10 電車は混むので互いに譲り合わないと。
Trains can be so crowded; we should be considerate to each other.

---

3. 電車が止まる・遅れる

01 最近は人身事故で電車が遅れることが多いですね。
We often face train delays recently due to accidents resulting in injury or death.

---

02 最近は電車の事故が多いです。
There are so many train accidents nowadays.

---

03 電車の事故が起こると、振替輸送があります。
We are able to use alternative means of transportation free of charge when there is a train accident.

---

04 先日は、架線事故で乗っていた電車が止まりました。
The other day I was on a train when one of the overhead power lines broke, causing the train to stop.

---

05 暑い中数時間も中に閉じ込められて気分が悪くなりました。
I was stuck inside the hot car for hours and began to feel sick.

No. 11

Chapter 2　Work

接待する

Entertaining clients

1. 接待する

01 明日は接待ゴルフです。
I have to take my clients to golf tomorrow.

02 週末はよく接待ゴルフで家族に嫌がられています。
I often have to take my clients golfing on weekends, and my family hates it.

03 よく接待でかなり飲まなければならないことがあります。
I often have to drink a lot with my clients.

04 接待じゃ、楽しめませんね。
We can't really enjoy ourselves when entertaining our clients.

05 接待では、飲まなくちゃなりませんが、酔うのは厳禁ですよ。
You have to drink when you are entertaining your clients, but you must never get drunk.

06 接待じゃ、酒を飲んでも酔えませんね。
You may drink, but can't relax, when you are entertaining your clients.

07 カラオケはどうですか。
How would you like to go to a *karaoke* bar?

---

08 カラオケは外国人のお客様にも結構受けますよ。
We found out that clients from overseas enjoy singing *karaoke*, too.

---

09 アメリカでは、クライアントの家に招かれて接待を受けました。
In the United States, I sometimes got invited to a client's home to be entertained.

---

2. 食事に気を配る

01 外国からのお客さんの中には、ベジタリアンもいらっしゃるので接待の時には注意が必要です。
We must be careful when we are entertaining guests from overseas because some of them may be vegetarians.

---

02 コーシャーフードでなければといけない人もいますからね。
We should know some people eat only kosher food: specially prepared food items for Jewish people.

接待に関するやりとり

A: 今夜は料亭大倉屋にお席を設けさせていただいております。

We've reserved a table for you at a traditional Japanese restaurant, Ookuraya, tonight.

お忙しいと存じますが、今夜は是非お付き合いいただきたく。

We know you are very busy, but please do accept our invitation to dinner tonight.

今夜は我々のご招待ということで。

It would be our pleasure to treat you to dinner tonight.

B: では、遠慮なく御馳走になります。

We appreciate your invitation.

A: お迎えのタクシーがまいりました。ホテルまでお送りいたします。

We have a taxi ready to take you back to your hotel.

本日はお忙しいところ、ご足労いただきありがとうございます。

We thank you so much for taking time out of your busy schedule to join us tonight.

B: 大変御馳走になりました。

Thank you for the wonderful [gorgeous] dinner tonight.

お土産までいただいてしまいまして、大変恐縮です。

I must thank you for the gift as well.

■食事に気を配る表現

召し上がれないものはありますか。

Is there anything you are not allowed to or prefer not to eat?

刺身やすしは大丈夫ですか。

Do you like *sashimi* and *sushi*?

11 接待する

どうぞご遠慮なく、何でもお好きなものを。
Feel free to take anything you like.

日本食で良いですか、それとも西洋料理にしますか。
Can we take you to a Japanese restaurant, or would you prefer Western-style food?

てんぷらやしゃぶしゃぶをお勧めします。
I recommend *tempura*, deep-fried battered shrimps and vegetables; or *Shabu-shabu*, thinly-sliced meat and vegetables cooked lightly in a broth and eaten with special sauces.

Chapter 3

自分の時間を過ごす

Free time

会話を盛り上げ、
自分のことを相手に伝える
「自分の時間」の使い方。

No. 01

Chapter 3　Free time

外食をする

Eating out

1. レストランに行く

01 今晩は外食です。
We're going out for dinner tonight.

02 二日前、駅前に高級なスペイン料理のレストランがオープンしました。
A fancy Spanish restaurant opened in front of the station two days ago.

03 うちは子ども連れなので、ファミリーレストランの方が気楽です。
Casual dining restaurants are more relaxing for us with small children.

04 明日の晩、7時に5人で予約しました。
I made a reservation for five at 7 o'clock tomorrow evening.

05 禁煙席はありません。
They don't offer non-smoking tables.

06 窓側の席をお願いしました。
I asked them to give us a table by the window.

Note：「(屋外の) テラス席」は on the terrace.

07 夫の誕生日に海の見えるレストランを予約しました。
For my husband's birthday, I made a reservation at a restaurant with a view of the sea.

08 そのフランス料理店は特別な地元ワインをそろえていることで知られています。
That French restaurant is known for its special selection of local wines.

09 有名なレストランなのに、お勘定が間違っていました。
At such a famous restaurant, there was a mistake in the bill.

10 タバコの煙が苦手なので、分煙の店に行きたいです。
Cigarette smoke really bothers me, so I'd like to go to a place that has a non-smoking section.

2. ファーストフード・ファミレスに行く

01 子どもたちはファーストフードが大好きです。
Our children love fast food.

02 ファーストフードレストランは子どもと母親で混んでいます。
Fast food restaurants are full of mothers and children.

03 チーズバーガーと大きいサイズのコーラを持ち帰りにしてください。
One cheeseburger and a large Coke to go, please.

04 ファミリーレストランに行くといつもドリンクバーを注文して何時間も粘ります。

When we go eat at what we call "family restaurants" in Japan, we always order bottomless drinks and stay in the restaurant for hours over tea and soft drinks.

Note：おかわり自由のドリンクバーは drinks with free refills とも。

3. 居酒屋に行く

01 私はいつも生ビールで始めます。
I always start with draft [tap] beer.

02 私の好みは黒ビールです。
My favorite is stout [dark] beer.

03 その居酒屋はいろんな種類の地ビールを出してくれます。
The pub serves a variety of local beers.

04 私はカクテル、特にドライ・マティーニに目がありません。
I love cocktails, especially a dry martini.

05 私はバーボンの水割り［スコッチのソーダ割り］を注文しました。
I ordered bourbon and water [Scotch and soda].

Note：「焼酎の水割り」は *shochu* and water.

06 兄はめっぽう酒に強く、いつもスコッチのストレートかオンザロックです。
My big brother is a heavy drinker and always orders Scotch straight or on the rocks.

07 「俺のつけにしてくれ」って言えたらなあ。
I wish I could say, "Put it on my tab."

---

08 各地の日本酒を飲み比べるのが好きです。
I love to drink local *sake* [Japanese rice wine] from different regions.

---

09 甘口、辛口など、様々な味わいの日本酒があります。
We can get a wide variety of *sake* [Japanese rice wine] with different flavors; some are sweet, and others dry.

---

10 梅酒は甘口で飲みやすく、女性に人気があります。
***Umeshu* or plum wines are usually sweet and easy to drink. They are popular especially among ladies.**

飲みに誘う

A： 今日帰りに一杯どうですか？
How about a drink after work?

B： そうだね。暑いからビアガーデンはどう？
That sounds good! It's been so hot today. So, how about a beer garden?

01 外食をする　149

4. 喫茶店に入る

01 毎朝地元のカフェにでかけて、「本日のコーヒー」を注文します。
I go to a local coffeehouse every morning and order the coffee of the day.

02 アップルパイを注文するときは温めてもらいます。
When I buy a piece of apple pie, I ask them to warm it up.

03 私はセルフサービスのコーヒーショップより落ち着いた喫茶店の方が好きです。
I prefer a tearoom with a calm atmosphere to a self-service coffee shop.

04 この店は 24 時間営業です。
This shop is open around the clock [24 hours a day].

05 ランチのための軽食もあります。
They serve light meals for lunch.

06 ホイップクリームののったコーヒーを注文したのに、出てきたのは泡立てた牛乳がのったものでした。
I ordered a coffee with whipped cream on it, but they served one with foamed milk.

No. 02

Chapter 3　Free time

ショッピングをする

Shopping

1. 店で買い物をする

01 これを試着していいですか。
May I try this on?

02 そのドレスは私にはちょっときつかったです。
The dress was a little too tight on me.

03 その商品を返品して、お金を返してもらいました。
I returned the item for a refund.

04 現金［クレジットカード］で払いました。
I paid (in) cash [by credit card].

05 もっと明るい色の服を置いてほしいです。
I wish they would sell [carry] brighter colored clothes [outfits].

06 年齢が上がり、自分に似合う服がないと感じます。
I'm no longer very young and find it more difficult to find clothes that fit [suit / look good on] people of my age.

07 仕事用のストッキングはスーパーでまとめ買いします。
I buy the inexpensive stockings that I wear to work in bulk at the supermarket.

---

08 服は量販店で購入します。
I buy my clothes at mass retailers.

---

09 バッグはブランド品を使っています。
When it comes to handbags [purses], I buy fancy, designer bags.

---

10 今年はコートを3着も買ってしまいました。
I bought THREE coats this year [season].

---

11 つい同じような服を買ってしまいます。
I tend to purchase similar-looking outfits.

---

12 げた箱に靴が入りきりません。
I've got too many pairs of shoes to fit in my shoe cupboard.

2. ネットショッピングをする

01 私のように忙しい人には、ネットショッピングはとても便利です。
Online shopping is very convenient for a busy person like me.

---

02 本や家電製品、洋服、化粧品は、たいていお気に入りのネットショッピングサイトで買います。
I usually buy books, electrical appliances, clothes and cosmetics from my favorite online shopping sites.

03 最初は、商品が壊れていたらどうしようと心配でした。
When I first tried online shopping, I was a bit worried I might receive a faulty product.

---

04 欠陥品や間違った商品は送料を負担せずにお金を払い戻してもらえます。
I can return a faulty or wrong item and get a full refund without paying the shipping cost.

---

05 気が変わったときも返せますが、送料はこちらの負担です。
When I simply change my mind, I can return the item, but I have to pay postage.

---

06 正直に言って、クレジットカードの番号を書き込むのには抵抗があります。
Honestly speaking, I don't like to input my credit card number.

---

07 近所に店がないので、買い物はほとんどネット通販です。
I live in an area where there are hardly any shops, so I usually shop online.

---

08 ペットボトルの水を定期的に家に届けてもらいます。
I have bottled drinking water delivered to my home regularly.

---

09 ネットで買い物をする人が増え、宅配便の配達員は本当に忙しそうです。
I can tell that a growing number of online shoppers are keeping home delivery service people really busy.

No. 03

Chapter 3　Free time

出かける

Going out

1. 旅行に行く

01 家族で東京から日帰りバス旅行で日光に行きました。
Our family took a one-day bus tour from Tokyo to Nikko.

02 妻と箱根の温泉旅館で1泊しました。
My wife and I enjoyed a one-night stay at a Japanese style inn with hot spring in Hakone.

03 このパック旅行はホテルと鉄道3日間乗り放題がついていてとてもお得でした。
This tour package was a good buy because it included a hotel room and a three-day free rail pass.

04 ヨーロッパ6泊7日 [7泊8日] 旅行のための荷造りで忙しいです。
I'm busy packing for a week-long trip [an 8-day trip] to Europe now.

05 初めて海外に行ったのは新婚旅行です。
I traveled abroad for the first time on my honeymoon.

06 私のパスポートはあと5年間有効です。
My passport is valid for another five years [for five more years].

---

07 時差ボケで眠いです。
I feel drowsy because of jet lag.

---

08 今年の夏は10日間の休暇を取ってフランスをあちこち旅行しました。
I took ten days off this summer and traveled around France.

---

09 ハワイに行ってゴルフを楽しんで来ました。
I enjoyed golfing in Hawaii.

---

10 私は一人で海外旅行をしたいと思います。
I'd like to travel abroad alone.

---

11 学生の間に海外旅行へ行きたいと思います。
I would like to take a trip overseas before I start working.

---

12 夏休みは人気のキャンプ場が学生でいっぱいです。
During the summer vacation, most of the popular campsites are full of students.

---

13 家族で海へ遊びに行きます。
We have family outings to the beach.

---

14 海でスイカ割りをします。
On the beach, we take turns trying to crack a watermelon open with a stick while blindfolded.

15 週末は軽井沢の［伊豆にある海辺の］別荘で過ごします。
We spend weekends at our holiday home in Karuizawa [near the ocean in Izu].

2. テーマパークに行く

01 人気の乗り物に乗るには列に並ばなければなりませんでした。
We had to wait in line for popular rides.

02 娘はジェットコースターがお気に入りです。
My daughter loves riding roller coasters.

03 入場券を買うのに時間がかかります。
It takes time to buy admission tickets.

04 人ごみで彼女とはぐれてしまったので、呼び出してもらいました。
I lost my girlfriend in the crowd, and I had her paged.

3. 映画を観る

01 私はホラー映画が大好きです。
I love horror films.

Note：スリラー a thriller ／コメディ a comedy ／恋愛もの a romantic film.

02 最高の映画でした。
It is the best movie I've ever seen.

03 主演はスウェーデン人の女優［俳優］です。
A Swedish actress [actor] plays the main role.

04　フランスのドキュメンタリー映画で英語の字幕がついています。
It's a French documentary film with English subtitles.

05　良いという評判だけれど、私には退屈だった。
I had heard it was a good movie, but I thought it was boring.

> Note：「アニメ映画」と言う場合、海外のアニメ映画 animated movies に対して日本のアニメは "anime". 「アニメ」と同様、漫画についても海外のコミック（「アメコミ」など）は comic books と言うのに対して、"manga" は日本の漫画を指す。

4. カラオケに行く

01　カラオケではプライベートな空間で思い切り歌えます。
You can enjoy singing to your heart's content in your own private space.

02　音程を調節できるので、好きなように歌えます。
You can adjust the key of the song in the way you like.

03　エコーを効かせたりリズムを変えたりすることもできます。
You can use the echo function or change the rhythm.

04　歌詞はモニター画面にでます。
You can see the lyrics on a monitor display.

05　色でハイライトされた歌詞を追いかけるだけです。
You just follow the words highlighted in color.

06 ときどきは採点カラオケにも挑戦します。
I sometimes try the skill grading system.

07 飲み会の二次会はたいていカラオケです。
We usually go to a *karaoke* bar after our after-work parties.

遊びに誘う

A： 映画を観に行きましょう。
Let's go to a movie.

B： いいよ、何をやってるの？
Thanks. What's on now?

A： ハリウッド映画の超大作だよ。
It's a Hollywood blockbuster.

A： 今晩カラオケ行かない？
Want to go sing *karaoke* tonight?

B： ごめん、他の人たちの前で歌うのは苦手で。
Thanks, but I don't like to sing in front of other people.

5. スポーツ観戦に行く

01 今晩の巨人・中日戦のチケットを2枚手に入れました。
I got two tickets for tonight's game between the Giants and the Dragons.

02 試合は後楽園球場で午後6時スタートです。
The game will start at 6 p.m. at Korakuen Stadium.

03 三塁側の内野席がまだ空いていました。
Some infield seats on the third base line were still available.

04 私はサッカーファンで、いつもJリーグの試合のスケジュールを調べています。
I am a soccer fan. I always check match schedules of the J. League.

6. 美容院・理髪店に行く

01 家の近くによい美容院があります。
There is a good beauty salon near my house.

02 私の美容師はとてもセンスの良い人で、信頼しています。
My hairdresser has good taste, so I trust her judgement.

03 水曜日の朝10時にカットとブローの予約をしました。
I made an appointment for a haircut and blow-dry for 10 a.m. Wednesday morning.

04 昨日パーマをかけたら2時間かかりました。
I got a perm yesterday. It took two hours.

05 パーマはゆるめ［きつめ］が好きです。
I prefer a soft [tight] perm.

06 そろそろ散髪にいかなければなりません。
I have to go to the barbershop soon.

07 前より横をすこし短くしました。
I got my hair cut a little shorter on the sides than before.

08 毛先［もみあげ］を そろえるよう頼みました。
I asked him to trim the ends [sideburns].

No. 04

Chapter 3　Free time

趣味を楽しむ

Other interests

1. 音楽を楽しむ

01 金管楽器ならほとんどなんでもできます。
I can play almost any brass instrument.

02 私のお気に入りのバンドはビートルズです。
My favorite band is the Beatles.

03 生の音楽を聞くのはもっとも楽しい経験の一つです。
Hearing live music is one of the most pleasurable experiences.

04 仕事の息抜きに昨日は音楽会に行ってきました。
I went to a concert yesterday to get away from my work.

05 明日のチャリティコンサートの席を3つ予約しておきました。
I have reserved three seats for tomorrow's charity concert.

06 昨夜のコンサートは大成功でした。
The concert last night was a great success.

07 音楽を聴く際は、CDの音源をMP3データに変換してスマホで聞いています。

I transfer music on CDs to MP3 data format and then listen to it on my smartphone.

---

08 よく音楽CDをレンタルします。

I usually rent music CDs at a rental shop.

---

09 音楽業界ではCDが売れなくなりましたが、ライブやイベントの人気は高まっています。

Music CDs are not selling well nowadays, but live concerts and meet-and-greets and the like are gaining popularity.

Note：meet-and-greetとは有名人に直接会ったり話したりできるイベントを指す。日本で言うところの「握手会」や「トークイベント」のようなものに近い。

---

2. 絵画を楽しむ

01 油絵を習っています。

I'm taking an oil painting lesson.

Note：水彩画は watercolor painting.

---

02 晴れた日はよくスケッチに出かけます。

I usually go sketching on a sunny day.

---

03 家の近くの美術館に今、あの有名なモナリザの絵が展示されています。

At a museum near my house, the famous Mona Lisa is being displayed now.

04 近代美術館のピカソ展は今月末までやっています。
The Picasso exhibition at the Museum of Modern Art will run until the end of this month.

05 ピカソの大作 10 作品が展示されています。
Picasso's ten masterpieces are on display.

06 最近はインターネットを通じて誰でも自分の絵を公開することができます。
Anyone can post their drawings [paintings] on the Internet for public viewing nowadays.

3. 手芸をする

01 妻は洋裁を習っています。
My wife is taking dressmaking lessons.

02 私のシャツのボタンが取れかかっているのを見て娘がつけてくれました。
My daughter found a button coming off my shirt and fixed it.

03 姉はミシンを使って古いドレスのリメークをしています。
My older sister is using a sewing machine to remake her old dresses.

04 彼女が私の誕生日に手編みの手袋をプレゼントしてくれました。
My girlfriend gave me hand-knit gloves on my birthday.

05 最近母はレース編みにこっています。
These days, my mother is crazy about lacework.

---

06 娘がピアノの稽古バッグにお花のアップリケをしてほしいと言っています。
My daughter has asked me to sew a flower appliqué onto a bag she takes to her piano lesson.

---

4. 習い事をする

生け花

01 「生け花」は花を生ける日本の芸術です。
***Ikebana* is the Japanese art of flower arrangement.**

---

02 日本の生け花は天、地、人を表す三つの層から構成されると教わりました。
I was taught that the Japanese flower arrangement is made of three layers, the sky at the top, the earth at the bottom and people in the middle.

---

03 週に一回公民会の生け花教室に通っています。
I'm taking an *ikebana* lesson once a week at the community center.

---

04 私は草月流の師範の免状を持っています。
I have a certificate to teach *ikebana* from the Sogetsu School.

茶道

01 私は夫と一緒に茶道を習っています。
I am learning tea ceremony with my husband.

02 お茶を飲む前に少しお茶碗を上げて感謝の気持ちを表します。
You raise the tea bowl slightly before drinking the tea to express your feeling of thanks.

03 薄茶は点てられるようになりましたが、濃茶はもっと難しいです。
I've learned how to make thin tea, but making thick tea is more difficult.

04 「和敬清寂」は茶道のもっとも重要な四つの要素だと言われます。
It is said that the four most important elements of tea ceremony are harmony, respect, purity and tranquility.

05 私は茶道を通して日本の様々な芸術や精神文化を学びたいと思います。
I hope I can learn various Japanese arts and philosophical principles through tea ceremony.

No. 05

Chapter 3　Free time

勉強する

Studying

1. 進学する

01 少なくとも 10 校受験します。
I will take the entrance examinations for at least 10 universities.

---

02 できるだけ多く模擬試験を受けます。
I will go through practice tests as many times as possible.

---

03 大学受験の準備で予備校に通っています。
I'm taking classes at a cram school to prepare for university entrance examinations.

---

04 大学付属の高校に通っています。
I'm attending a private high school that is affiliated with a university.

---

05 今の高校のクラスであまりにひどい成績を取らない限り、系列の大学には入れると思います。
Unless I do extremely poorly in my classes at my current high school, my position in the affiliated university is secured.

06 ロースクールに進むつもりです。
I intend to go to law school.

---

07 一生懸命勉強しないとK大学の医学部には進めません。
I have to study really hard to pass the exam to enter K University School of Medicine.

---

08 2校ぐらいAO入試に応募するかもしれません。
I might apply for an AO admission [a special admission] at a couple of colleges.

Note：AO入試に直接対応する英語はない。

---

09 AO受験をする場合は、英語で作文を書かされるかもしれません。
I may have to write an essay in English if I want to apply to a college through the AO admission [the special admission] process.

---

10 英語での授業を実施している大学を受験することも考えています。
I'm thinking about applying to a university which offers courses in English.

---

11 博物学［物理 / 英文学 / 心理学］をやりたいと思います。
I would like to study natural history [physics / English literature / psychology].

---

12 防衛大学校を受験しようかと思います。
I think I will apply to the National Defense Academy.

13 どこかから奨学金をもらいたいです。
I would like to get some kind of scholarship.

14 日本学生支援機構に育英資金を申し込もうと思っています。
I think I will apply to JASSO, the Japan Student Services Organization, for a student loan.

2. 英語を学ぶ

01 うちの会社では、英語が公用語なので、どうしても英語が話せるようにならないといけないのです。
I must learn to speak English, since that is the official means of communication in our company.

02 リスニングはかなり力が付いてきたと思います。
I think my listening comprehension has improved a lot.

03 英語は国際語ですね。
I think we can say English is THE global means of communication now.

04 大学受験の時に勉強した英語の文法や語彙が役に立っていますよ。
I can tell the English grammar and vocabulary I learned when I was studying for university entrance exams are now paying off.

05 最近は、朝、会社へ行く前に「英語で朝食会」という会合にできるだけ出るようにしています。

Recently, I've been trying to join a group called "a Breakfast in English" before I go to my office as often as possible.

---

06 大学では毎日、英語でランチという会があり、ネイティブの先生たちと会話を楽しんでいます。

We have a lunch-in-English session every day at our university, where I enjoy talking with native English-speaking teachers over lunch.

---

07 海外にいる友人と、スカイプでよく話します。

I often talk to my friends overseas over Skype.

---

3. 英語の試験を受ける

01 TOEFL［TOEIC］の点数を上げるために英語を勉強しています。

I'm studying English to get a better score on the TOEFL [TOEIC].

---

02 TOEIC のリスニングの点数を上げたいんです。

I want to improve my score on the listening section of the TOEIC test.

---

03 会社でさらなる昇進の資格を得るため、次回の TOEIC 試験では必ず 900 点以上を取る決意でいます。

I'm determined to get a score of more than 900 on TOEIC next time I take it to qualify for further promotion in my company.

04 来月、日本政府観光局が実施する通訳案内士試験で良い点を取るために、高校時代の地理の教科書を勉強し直しています。

I'm revisiting the geography textbook from my high school years so I can do well on the interpreter-guide examination conducted by the JNTO [Japan National Tourism Organization] next month.

4. 外国語を学ぶ

01 韓国語を勉強し始めました。

I've started to learn the Korean language.

02 韓国語は文法も語彙も結構日本語とよく似ていて、学びやすいです。

I find it rather easy to learn Korean, since it has similar grammar and vocabulary to those of Japanese.

03 うちの会社では、中国に生産拠点を構えているので、中国語は、必須です。

We must learn Chinese because our company has a production base in China.

04 中国語は、四声がすごく難しいです。

I find the Chinese four tones are extremely difficult to learn.

05 中国語は、漢字である程度意味が分かるので、助かります。

Luckily, with Chinese characters, we can understand the meaning to some extent.

06 手話を学んでいます。
I am learning sign language.

Note：国際手話 the international sign language.

5. 運転免許をとる

01 運転免許を取るために自動車学校に通っています。
I'm going to driving school in order to get my (driver's) license.

02 免許を取るために2週間の合宿に行きました。
I learned to drive at a 2-week driving camp in order to get my license.

03 もうすぐ卒業検定です。
I will be taking the final driving test soon.

04 オートマ（AT）限定の免許を取りました。
I got a driver's license only good for driving a vehicle with an automatic transmission.

05 実家の車がマニュアル車なのでマニュアル（MT）で免許を取りました。
My family owns a car with a manual transmission, so I got a license that allows me to drive one.

Note：「マニュアル車を運転できます」I can drive a manual. / I can drive a stick (shift).

06 よく坂道でエンストしてしまいます。
I often experience engine failures when driving uphill.

05 勉強する

6. 留学する

01 この大学にいる間に、少なくとも1年は留学したいです。
I want to study abroad at least a year while I am still a student here at this university.

02 授業料や生活費などとても費用がかかります。
The tuition and living costs will be very expensive.

03 A大学では、1年間の授業料と入学金で13,000ドル以上かかるとわかりました。
I found out that the tuition and fees at A University will be more than $13,000 a year.

04 カナダにある大学の姉妹校で、来年夏に英語を勉強するチャンスをもらいました。
I will have a chance to study English at one of our university's sister colleges in Canada next summer.

05 大学の交換留学の制度について調べています。
I'm checking on the exchange student program offered by our university.

06 ロンドン大学東洋アフリカ研究学院でEUについて研究したいと思っています。
I would like to do research on the European Union at SOAS [the School of Oriental and African Studies], University of London.

07 韓国語を専攻していて、ソウルの延世大学で韓国の古代史を勉強したいと思っています。

I'm majoring in Korean and want to study the ancient history of the country at Yonsei University in Seoul.

---

08 中国語はビジネスでも役立つと思いますので、北京大学に中国語を学びに留学したいです。

I think the Chinese language would be very useful now in doing business. So I want to study the language at Peking University.

---

09 大学からの入学許可を待っています。

I'm waiting for a letter of admission from the university.

---

10 アメリカ領事館へ学生ビザの申請に行かなくてはなりません。

I have to go to the US Consulate to apply for a student visa.

---

11 奨学金に応募して留学費用の一部を賄えるかもしれません。

I may be able to apply for a scholarship to pay for part of the cost of my education abroad.

---

12 親に経済的な支援を頼まないといけないかもしれません。

I may have to ask my parents to help me financially.

13 ロンドンに赴任中の夫に同伴してきたので、私自身、ロンドンの大学院で MBA を取りたいと思います。

While I'm living in London with my husband who is stationed here now, I might as well go to a graduate school here to get an MBA myself.

---

7. 会社の留学制度を利用する

01 会社の1年間の留学制度に応募します。

I will apply for a year-long study abroad program offered by our company.

---

02 会社が有望な従業員に提供している留学制度で奨学金に応募しています。

I applied for a scholarship our company provides to promising employees so that they can study abroad.

---

03 会社が実施しているフィリピンのマニラでの奨学金付き英語留学の選抜試験を来月受けます。

I will take the screening tests for a scholarship given by our company to study English in Manila, the Philippines, next month.

---

04 会社から奨学金をもらえたら、マニラで3カ月英語を勉強します。

If I get the scholarship provided by the company, I will study English in Manila for 3 months.

8. 大学に再び通う・博士号を取得する

01 また大学に戻っていろいろクラスをとりたいです。
I want to go back to college [university] and take various classes.

02 大学生の時は遊んでばかりいました。
I fooled around a lot when I was a university student.

03 いろいろ知的刺激のある生活がしたいです。
I want to live a life with a lot of intellectual stimulation.

04 最初の大学時代とは、まったく畑違いのロシア文学が勉強したいのです。
I want to study Russian literature, which is a discipline completely different from what I studied when I went to college the first time.

05 既に社会学の学士号は持っています。
I already have a BA in sociology.

06 家庭の事情で大学に行きそびれました。
Due to my family circumstances, I was not able to get a university education.

07 夜間の大学に行くつもりです。
I plan to go to night school.

08 昼間は働いているので、夜のクラスを2科目履修しています。
I work during the day, so I am taking 2 night classes.

09 ずいぶん年下の若者と一緒に机を並べて、また勉強するのもすごく楽しいです。

I am enjoying my second time in college immensely, studying with much younger students.

---

10 インターネットでいろいろな授業を提供している海外の大学のコースも取れます。

We can take a number of courses offered by some overseas universities via the Internet.

---

11 働きながら学校に戻って勉強するのは、大変ですが、楽しいと思います。

I think it is fun to go back to school while you work, though it is challenging.

---

12 働きながらの博士号の取得には7年かかりました。

It took me seven years to obtain a doctor's degree because I worked my way through college.

再入学・仮面浪人

5年間勤めた会社を辞めて、地方の国立大学の医学部に入学しました。

　I quit the firm where I worked for 5 years and entered medical school at a national university outside Tokyo.

K大学で仮面浪人をしたあと、本命のW大学に入学しました。

　I went to K University, which was not my first choice, to prepare for the entrance examination to W University, which is the one I wanted to attend. I was lucky enough to get admitted to W University in the end.

9. 生涯学習で見識を高める

01 いろいろな大学のエクステンションセンターで、さまざまな授業が行われています。
Many universities' extension centers are offering various courses.

02 大学のエクステンションセンターのクラスは、年齢や資格に関係なく、誰でも受講できます。
Those classes offered by university extension centers are open to anyone, regardless of their age or qualifications.

03 T大学のエクステンションセンターで、古事記とフィンランド語のクラスを取っています。
I am taking classes on *Kojiki*, or the Records of Ancient Matters of Japan, and the Finnish language at T University's extension.

04 いろいろな資格を取れる通信講座もありますよ。
We can take all kinds of correspondence courses for different qualifications.

05 ファイナンシャル・プランナーの講座を取りました。
I took a course to be a certified financial planner.

No. 06

Chapter 3　Free time

情報を収集する

Getting information

1. インターネットを活用する

01 外で食事をする時は、ネットで近くの人気店を調べます。
When I want to eat out, I go online and look up popular restaurants in the area.

02 アマゾンで買い物をする時は、必ずカスタマー・レビューをチェックします。
I always check the customer reviews when I purchase something on Amazon.

03 カスタマー・レビューはすごく参考になります。
I find the customer reviews very helpful.

04 渋谷のレストランでのディナーに行くのに、ネットで割引クーポンをゲットしました。
I got a discount ticket for dinner at a restaurant in Shibuya on the Internet.

05 よく「ぐるなび」でレストランを選びます。
I often use "Gurunavi," a gourmet restaurant guide, when choosing a restaurant.

インターネットの問題点

ネットに不用意に情報をアップロードし、不特定多数の人に情報が拡散されてしまう事例もあります。

You can upload information and have it spread to anyone and everyone without intending to do so, unless you are careful.

時にはネットを通じて個人が激しいバッシングを受けることもあります。

We sometimes see individuals bashed badly on the Internet.

インターネット上に不用意に個人情報を掲載しないほうがよいでしょう。

You should not upload personal information on the Internet carelessly.

2. スマホやタブレットを使う

01 最近は移動中によく携帯でインターネットの情報を取得します。

I often get information on the Internet using my mobile while I'm on the go.

02 スマホがあれば、電車の運賃の支払いから銀行振り込みまで、何でも用が足ります。

I can do almost anything with my smartphone, from paying for a train ride to sending money from my bank account.

03 携帯で新幹線の席の予約をします。

I use my cell phone to reserve a seat on a bullet train.

04 スマホなしの生活は考えられません。

I can't imagine life without a smartphone.

05 最近はスマホ中毒の人もいるらしいですよ。
I understand there are some people addicted to smartphones nowadays.

06 スマホを手から離すと本当に文字通り気分が悪くなる人がいるとか。
I hear some people start feeling literally sick if they let go of their smartphones.

07 会社訪問や面接の予約は、スマホでします。
We use smartphones to make an appointment for a company visit or an interview.

08 私は方向音痴なので、スマホのマップはすごく便利です。
I have a poor sense of direction, so I find the map application on my smartphone very useful.

09 携帯で毎週［毎月］のスケジュール管理をするようになりました。
I now manage my weekly [monthly] schedule on my mobile.

10 やはり手帳でスケジュール管理するのが好きです。
I still like to manage my schedule in my schedule book.

11 カバーの選択肢が多いので、iPhone にしました。
I switched to an iPhone because I liked the variety of cases I could choose from.

12 いまだにガラケー［二つ折りの携帯電話］を使っています。
I'm still using a dumbphone [a flip phone].

Note：日本の「ガラケー」に近いのは dumbphone（ダムホン、単純携帯）.

13 この間、スマホに夢中になっていて、危うくホームから落ちるところでした。

Just the other day, I was so busy looking at my smartphone that I almost stepped off of the platform at the station.

---

14 わかっているんですが、ついつい歩きながらスマホを使っちゃいますね。

I know I shouldn't do it, but I can't stop myself from using my smartphone while walking.

---

15 事故を起こす前に「歩きスマホ」は止めないといけないです。

I should stop using my smartphone while walking, before I cause an accident.

---

3. LINE・ツイッターを利用する

01 友人とは LINE で連絡を取っています。LINE というのは日本で人気のあるチャットと通話ができるアプリです。

I contact my friends by LINE, which is one of the most popular apps for chats and calls in Japan.

Note：「アプリ」は application. 会話では app も使われる。

---

02 LINE は送ったメッセージが読まれたかどうかを知らせてきます。

LINE lets you know if your messages have been read or not.

---

03 日本はツイッターの利用者がとても多いと言われています。

I hear Japan has a large number of Twitter users.

04 多くの企業、新聞社がツイッターを通して最新の情報を発信しています。

Many firms and newspaper publishers offer the latest news and information on Twitter.

05 非常時［災害時］には一般の人のツイート（つぶやき）を通じて情報を得られます。

You can get necessary [useful] information via ordinary people's Tweets at the time of an emergency [a disaster].

4. 本を読む

01 書籍をネットで買う人が増え、書店で買う人が減っています。

More and more people buy books on the Internet nowadays, and fewer and fewer are buying at bookshops.

02 私は書店で本を買うようにしています。

I choose to go and buy books at a bookstore.

03 本は手にとって選びたいですね。

I love to hold books in my hand before I choose which to buy.

04 1週間に1度は、会社の帰りに書店に行くのが楽しみです。

I enjoy dropping by a bookstore on the way home from work at least once a week.

05 電子書籍は、かさばらないし、安くていいですよ。

I like e-books because they are not bulky and are less expensive.

06 電子書籍を読むのに、iPad ミニにキンドルのアプリをダウンロードしました。

I downloaded the Kindle application on my iPad mini to read e-books.

---

07 でも、やはり最新の本は、まだ本屋に行って買います。

I still go to a bookstore to buy the latest books.

---

08 最近は座るところがある本屋もあり、ゆったりできますよ。

We can relax at some of the bookstores nowadays because they have a space to sit down in.

---

09 今年の直木賞を受賞した小説を読んでいます。

I'm reading the novel that won this year's *Naoki* Award.

---

5. テレビを観る

01 忙しくて、なかなかテレビを観る時間がありません。

I'm very busy and do not have much time to watch television nowadays.

---

02 好きな番組を、よくオンデマンドで観ます。

I often use the on-demand TV program service to watch what I like.

---

03 NHK の朝ドラは見逃しません。

I never miss NHK's morning drama.

04 よくBSでMLBやテニスの試合を観ます。
I often watch Major League Baseball games and tennis matches on BS.

6. 新聞を取る

01 東京新聞をとっています。
I get *the Tokyo* paper.

02 新聞の一部の記事はネットで読みます。
I read some news articles on the Internet.

03 ネットのニュース記事では、深みのある情報は得られません。
We can't get in-depth information on anything from news articles on the Internet version of papers.

04 解説記事は、やはり新聞で読みたいです。
I like to read think pieces in newspapers.

05 S新聞の毎週の特集記事を読むのが好きです。
I enjoy reading weekly feature articles in the S newspaper.

06 Y新聞の日本語版と英語版を読んで、ニュースの英語表現を勉強します。
I read the Y newspaper and its English version to learn expressions used in the news and their translation in English.

No. 07

Chapter 3 Free time

社会に参加する
Social responsibilities

1. 投票に行く

01 昨日の衆議院選挙では、私は平和党の鈴木さんに投票をしました。
In the Lower House election yesterday, I voted for Mr. Suzuki from the Peace Party.

02 初めて投票権を行使しました。
I exercised my right to vote for the first time.

03 投票日に仕事があるので、今日期日前投票をしてきました。
I have to work on voting day, so I cast an absentee ballot today.

04 投票率が低かったと聞いてがっかりです。
I'm disappointed to hear the voter turnout was very low.

05 今朝、投票所に出かけました。
I went to a polling station this morning.

06 私が応援した候補者が当選して嬉しいです。
I'm very happy because the candidate I supported won the election.

07 私の高校時代からの親友が知事選に立候補しています。

My close friend from my senior high school days is running in the gubernatorial election.

---

2. 祭りに参加する

01 毎年5月に八幡神社のお祭りがあります。

We celebrate an annual festival at the Hachiman Shrine in May.

---

02 お祭りの運営はうちの自治会に任されています。

Our neighborhood association is responsible for organizing the festival.

---

03 父はその神社の氏子の総代です。

My father is a representative of the shrine parishioners.

---

04 3年前から観光客にもおみこしを担いでもらうようにしています。

We have asked visitors to join us in carrying a portable shrine for the past three years.

---

05 お囃子の練習は2か月前ぐらいに始めます。

We start practicing the festival music about two months before the festival.

---

3. 社会奉仕をする

01 毎年誕生日が来ると、赤十字血液センターで献血しています。

Every year on my birthday, I donate blood at the Red Cross Blood Center.

02 3月11日の震災の被災地でボランティア活動をするつもりです。
I will be doing some volunteer work in the areas struck by the 3/11 disaster.

> Note : 3/11 の読み方は Three Eleven. 東日本大震災は The great East Japan Earthquake.

03 障害者のためのボランティア活動をしています。
I work as a volunteer to help people with disabilities.

04 このイベントは若いスポーツ選手を応援するための募金活動の一つです。
This event is one of the fund raising activities to support young athletes.

05 母は国際的な環境 NGO で広報活動の手伝いをしています。
My mother helps with public relations at an international NGO for environmental protection.

4. 政治活動をする

01 昨日、戦争反対のデモに参加しました。
I joined an anti-war demonstration yesterday.

02 私はある保守政党の青年部で活動しています。
I am an active member of the youth wing of a conservative political party.

03 税金値上げ反対の署名活動に参加しました。
I took part in a signature rally to protest a tax hike.

No. 08

Chapter 3　Free time

スポーツを楽しむ

Sports

1. テニスをする

01 良いプレイをするにはスタミナをつけなければいけません。
I have to build stamina to perform well.

02 うちの家から2キロほどのところにコートがあります。
There is a court just 2 kilometers away from our house.

03 妻はすごいサーブをします。
My wife has an amazing serve.

04 最後の試合で3回もダブルフォールトをしてしまいました。
I double-faulted three times in my last match.

05 東京には公共のコートが足りません。
We don't have enough public courts in Tokyo.

06 楽しくプレイできれば十分です。
I'm happy just playing for fun.

07 今日は4人集まったので、ダブルスをしましょう。
We have four players today. Let's play doubles.

2. ゴルフをする

01 明日、同僚たちとゴルフをします。
I will play golf with my colleagues tomorrow.

---

02 ゴルフの練習場によく行きます。
I often go to a driving range.

---

03 今日は 75 で回りました。
I played 75 today.

---

04 ワン・オーバー［スリー・アンダー］で終わりました。
I finished one over [three under] par.

---

05 ショートホールで 6 打たたきました。
On the par-three hole, I shot a six.

---

06 第 2 ホールでは、ボギーでした。
On the second hole, I made a bogey.

Note：パー a par ／バーディ a birdie ／イーグル an eagle.

---

07 夫はゴルフにかまけて、私をほったらかしです。
My husband is a golf addict, and I am a golf widow.

3. スキー・スノーボードをする

01 私たちは今週末スキーに行きます。
We're going skiing this weekend.

02 長いスロープを滑り降りると気分がスカッとします。
It's exciting to ski down a long slope.

03 娘が雪の吹き溜まりに突っ込んで足を折りました。
My daughter rammed into a snow bank and broke her leg.

04 今回が僕のスノボ初体験だった。
This was my first time snowboarding.

05 もう少し難しい斜面を滑ろう。
Let's try more challenging slopes.

06 私はたいていレンタルの板と靴を使っています。
I usually use rental skis and boots.

07 このスキーツアーには2日間のリフト代が含まれています。
This skiing tour package includes a two-day lift ticket.

08 私は初級者ゲレンデ専門です。
I stay on the beginner's slope.

09 早朝は雪が硬いのでスピードがでるでしょう。
You will gain speed early in the morning because the snow is hard.

4. スキューバダイビングをする

01 私たちは沖縄でガイド付きのダイビング・ツアーに行きました。
We took a guided diving tour in Okinawa.

02 ダイビングは初めてでした。
It was my first time to dive.

03 私のいとこはダイバーの資格を持っています。
My cousin is a certified diver.

04 たくさんの水中写真を撮りました。
I took a lot of underwater photos.

05 水はものすごく澄んでいました。
The water was crystal clear.

06 12メートルぐらい潜りました。
We descended about twelve meters deep.

07 耳に水が入って抜けません。
I cannot clear my ears.

Chapter 4

基本フレーズ

Basic phrases

自分の名前、出身、
趣味などを話す基本的な自己紹介と、
自分の名前の由来や星座など、
ちょっとしたひねりを加える
表現を紹介します。

Chapter 4 Basic phrases

自己紹介をする

Introducing yourself

1. 名前

01 私の名前は「幸子」です。
I am Sachiko, which means "a happy child."

---

02 私は 2000 年春 3 月の生まれです。
I was born in the spring, in March 2000.

---

03 娘を「桜」と名付けました。
We named our baby Sakura, which means cherry blossom.

---

2. ○○出身［所属］です

01 東京ディズニーランドで有名な千葉県浦安市の出身です。
I'm from Urayasu City in Chiba, which is famous for Tokyo Disneyland.

---

02 故郷の［住み慣れた町である、私の住んでいる］大洗は、海水浴場として有名です。
My hometown Oarai is a famous seaside [beach] resort.

> Note：英語の hometown は生まれ育った土地、住み慣れた土地、現在住んでいる場所のいずれをも意味する。

03 いつか遊びに来てくださいね。
Please come and see me sometime.

---

04 筑波大学出身です。
I am a graduate of Tsukuba University.

---

05 大学で工学を学んでいます。
I'm studying [majoring in] engineering at college [university].

---

06 教育社会学を専攻しています。
I'm majoring in the sociology of education.

Note：文学 literature ／理学 science ／経済学 economics.

---

07 （総合大学の）教養学部に通っています。
I'm in the College of Arts and Sciences.

---

08 大学では経営学を学びました。
I studied business administration [management] at college [university].

---

09 銀行で働いています。
I work in a bank.

3. 星座

A： あなたの星座は何ですか？
What sign are you? / What's your (star) sign?

B： てんびん座です。
(I'm (a)) Libra.

星座の言い方

- おひつじ座 Aries / the Ram
- おうし座 Taurus / the Bull
- ふたご座 Gemini / the Twins
- かに座 Cancer / the Crab
- しし座 Leo / the Lion
- おとめ座 Virgo / the Virgin
- てんびん座 Libra / the Balance / the Scales
- さそり座 Scorpio / the Scorpion
- いて座 Sagittarius / the Archer
- やぎ座 Capricorn / the Goat
- みずがめ座 Aquarius / the Water Bearer
- うお座 Pisces / the Fishes

4. 干支

A: 干支では何年の生まれですか［(あなたの) 干支は何ですか］？
What's your Chinese year? / What Chinese year were you born in? / What's your Chinese (zodiac) sign?

B: 戌年です。
I was born in the year of the Dog.

十二支

- 十二支 **the twelve signs of the Chinese zodiac**
- 子（ね）**the Rat, the Mouse**
- 丑（うし）**the Ox, the Cow**
- 寅（とら）**the Tiger**
- 卯（う）**the Rabbit, the Hare**
- 辰（たつ）**the Dragon**
- 巳（み）**the Serpent, the Snake**
- 午（うま）**the Horse**
- 未（ひつじ）**the Sheep**
- 申（さる）**the Monkey**
- 酉（とり）**the Cock, the Rooster**
- 戌（いぬ）**the Dog**
- 亥（い）**the Boar, the Pig**

自己紹介をする

Index 日本語索引

ページ数は日本語のキーワードに関連する表現が掲載されているページを示しています。
英語については、日本語での読み方をもとに配列しました。　例）MP3 →エムピースリー

あ

アイロン	012
あかぎれ	099
赤字	019
朝ドラ	183
アパート	046-047
アマゾン	178
歩きスマホ	181
アルバイト	104
アレルギー	042
アレルギー物質	016
暗証番号	020

い

胃潰瘍	043
胃カメラ	040
育児休暇［育休］	032, 130
育メン	067
生け花	077, 164
居酒屋	148
いじめ	037
イチゴ狩り	095
一戸建て	049
一般職	104, 137
居眠り	045
イヤイヤ期	033
医療費	021
医療保険	023
インフルエンザ	042, 099

う

ウェディングドレス	065
薄茶	165
梅酒	062, 149
売り手市場	105
上着	004
運休	056
運転免許	171
運動会	088-089, 113

え

エアコン	016, 097
映画	156-158
営業	107, 112-113, 131
ATS	054
エクステンションセンター	177
エコバッグ	010
干支	197
MBA	174
MP3	162
エンジニア	111-112
エンスト	171

お

追い炊き	047
お色直し	065
大型連休	084-085
OJT	119
大掃除	016-017, 091
オートマ	171
オートロック	047
大みそか	090-091
お食い初め	027
おせち	078, 091
お茶くみ	108-109
お年玉	079
お盆	027, 087
お見合い	063-064
おむつ	032-033, 036
おむつかぶれ	032
オリンピック	092-093
音楽	103, 161-162
温泉旅館	154
オンデマンド	183

か

絵画	162-163
介護	029-030, 125-126
介護福祉士	126
介護保険	029
外資系企業	107, 136
外食	007, 146-150
買い手市場	105
書き初め	077
学食	006
家計	019-021
家計簿	019
火災保険	023
家事分担	025
カスタマー・レビュー	178
家族葬	075
家庭裁判所	069
家庭内別居	068
家庭内暴力	070
可燃ゴミ	017-018
花粉症	096
仮面浪人	176
カラオケ	142, 157-158
ガラケー	180
かるた	077
過労死	133

198　Index

眼科	043	結婚式	029, 065-066, 071-072	ゴルフ	141, 155, 189
韓国語	170, 173	結膜炎	043	婚期	038
元旦	076	結露	016	コンビニ	007, 057, 074
観葉植物	062	ゲリラ豪雨	056	婚約	065
管理費［料金］	048-049	嫌煙	045		

き

		献花	073, 075	## さ	
起業	103, 125	献血	186	財産分与	069
期日前投票	185	健康保険	023, 132	祭日	083
帰省	025-026	健診	040-041	賽銭	076
喫煙	045	建ぺい率	049-050	在宅勤務	132
ぎっくり腰	043			再入学	175-176
喫茶店	150	## こ		茶道	165
きつね色	011			サラ金	023
忌引き	073	濃茶	165	三回忌	028
虐待	070	公共料金	020	産休	032
休肝日	007	高校野球	097	残業代	019
旧婚旅行	028	合コン	063	三種混合	033
旧姓	117	交際費	021	残暑	097
教育費	037	厚生年金	022, 132		
教員	105, 113-114	交通事故	056	## し	
狂犬病	059	香典	074-075		
共用部分	048	強盗	057	自家発電	054
去勢	061	公認会計士試験	105	敷金	048
義理チョコ	081	光熱費	021	時給	128-129
禁煙	045	紅白歌合戦	091	事業主	022
禁煙席	146	公務員	102, 109-110	資源ゴミ	018
金管楽器	161	公用語	168	時差ボケ	155
キンドル	183	公立中学校	037	四十九日	028
金利	050	コーシャーフード	142	地震	053-054
		コーディネート	005	自炊	008-009
## く		コーヒー	006, 150	四声	170
		コールセンター	110	自然分娩	031
クラブ活動	037	ゴールデン・ウィーク	084-085	下着	005
クリーニング	012			試着	151
クリスマス	089-090	小型犬	059	失業	126
ぐるなび	178	国際結婚	069	失業保険	126, 131
クレーム	110	国際離婚	070	湿疹	042
黒字	019	告別式	074-075	ジップロック	009
		国民健康保険	132	自動運転停止装置	054
## け		国民年金	132	自動車保険	023
		寿退社	124	シフト	111
経理	109	子どもの日	083-084	司法試験	105
敬老の日	087	粉ミルク	032	ジム	044
血液検査	040	ゴミ	017-018	事務職	107-108
欠航	056	ゴミ捨て場	017	社員食堂	006
結婚記念日	028	雇用保険	022	社員旅行	119-120
		娯楽費	021	社会福祉士	105

日本語索引　199

車検	052	新聞社	102, 182	掃除	015-017, 048, 060, 091
車庫証明	051	信用審査	050	掃除機	016-017
シャンプー	004			掃除ロボット	015
獣医	059	**す**		遭難者	056
衆議院選挙	185	Suica	139	雑煮	078
祝儀袋	072	推薦入試	039	粗大ゴミ	017-018
就職活動	104-106	睡眠薬	003		
修繕積立金	049	スーパー	009, 152	**た**	
住宅費	021	スカイプ	169	退院	043
住宅ローン	020, 050-051	スキー	190	ダイエット	044
柔軟剤	013	好き嫌い	007	大往生	030
十二支	197	スキューバダイビング	191	大学受験	039, 166-168
塾	038, 086	スクーター	052	退職	124-127
手芸	163-164	捨て猫	060	退職金	125-126
手術	044	スヌーズ	002	耐震性	049
出産予定日	031	スノーボード	190	台風	053
出身	194-195	スマホ［スマートフォン］		高潮	053
出世	136-137		045, 076, 162, 179-181	タキシード	065
手話	171			抱っこ	033
春闘	134	**せ**		建売住宅	049
生涯学習	177	生活費	021, 172	七夕	085
奨学金	020, 168, 173-174	税金	022-023, 187	ダニ	016
正月	076-079	税込	022	タバコ	045, 147
小学校	036, 055, 114	星座	195-196	誕生日	026-027, 147, 163, 186
正月休み	077	税抜	022	団体信用生命保険	050
昇給	134-135	精密検査	040	暖冬	099
消費者金融	023	税務申告	022	胆のう	040
消費税	022	生命保険	023, 050		
ショートステイ	029	生理	042	**ち**	
職業訓練	126	咳	042	地域猫	061
食材	010, 078	施主	073	知事選	186
触診	041	セダン	051	中学校	036-037, 114
嘱託	127	接待	141-144	中高一貫校	037
食費	020-021	接待ゴルフ	141	中国語	170, 173
食欲	042	選挙	109, 185	注文建築	049
所属	194-195	専業主婦	025, 067	超音波検査	040
食器洗い	009	選手村	092	朝食	004, 006
所得控除	023	洗濯	012-014	朝食会	169
所得税	022	洗濯機	012-013	チラシ	010
初任給	128	剪定	062	賃貸	046, 048, 059
署名	187				
除夜の鐘	091	**そ**		**つ**	
親権	069	葬儀	073-075	ツイッター	181-182
人身事故	140	総合職	104, 137	通勤	052, 138-140
浸水	055	早産	032		
震度	054				
新聞	184				

通信費	021
通訳案内士試験	170
突っ張り棒	054
津波	053
通夜	073, 075
梅雨	014, 096
つわり	031

て

DPT	033
帝王切開	031
定期健診	040-041
デイケア	029
停電	054
定年	126-127
テーマパーク	156
できちゃった婚	065
手取り	022, 048, 128
テニス	114, 184, 188
手羽先	011
デモ	187
電子書籍	182-183
転職	121-123, 136
点滴	044
天引き	022

と

トイレ	004, 043, 047
倒産	126
同性のパートナー	024
投票	185-186
投票率	185
TOEIC	169
TOEFL	169
独身	024, 065
特別養護老人ホーム	030
年越しそば	091
土砂崩れ	053
突風	055
留袖	071
共働き	025, 034-035
土用の丑の日	098
ドライアイ	045
ドラム式洗濯機	013
泥足	015

な

内定	037, 104-105
中州	055
夏休み	025, 086, 155
なでしこジャパン	094
生ゴミ	018

に

二次会	072, 158
24時間営業	150
二世帯住宅	067
ニット	013
二度寝	002
乳がん	041
尿検査	040
任意保険	051
妊娠	031
認知症	030

ね

寝起き	002
ネクタイ	005
寝正月	077
寝だめ	003
寝違え	043
熱帯魚	060
熱中症	053, 097
ネットショッピング	152-153
ネットニュース	184

の

ノーアイロン	012
野良猫	061
ノロウイルス	043

は

ハーグ条約	070
バージンロード	029
パート（タイム）	103, 115
パーマ	160
俳徊	030
倍返し	066
肺がん	044
墓参り	027, 087
吐き気	042
掃き掃除	016
博士号	175-176
派遣	115
バター	010
はたき	017
バツイチ	065
発症率	041
初宮参り	027
初もうで	076
初夢	077
花火	086
花見	095
バブル	047
歯磨き	004
春一番	095
バレンタイン	080-082
ハローワーク	126
半返し	066, 074
晩酌	007
パンツ	013

ひ

引き落とし	021
ひげそり	004
ビザ	173
秘書	108
非常勤講師	114
非常持ち出し袋	054
ひったくり	057
一人暮らし	024
一人っ子	024
ひな祭り	082-083
避難	053, 055
避妊	061
肥満	042
美容院	159-160
披露宴	066, 071-072
ぴんぴんころり	030

ふ

ファーストフード	147
ファミリーレストラン[ファミレス]	146-148

ブーケ	062
拭き掃除	016
福袋	078-079
福利厚生	130-133
不祝儀袋	074
不動産屋	048-049
布団	015-016
ブラック企業	117
振替輸送	054, 140
不倫	070
フルタイム	104, 115
フレックス	035, 131
風呂	002, 036, 047
分煙	147
文鳥	060
分娩	031

へ

平服	074-075
ベジタリアン	142
別居	066, 068
ペット	047, 059-060
ペットホテル	059
ペットロス	060
ヘビースモーカー	045
部屋干し	014
ベランダ	012, 061
返済額	050
弁当	006, 008-009
返品	151

ほ

保育園	034-035, 124, 131
保育士	113
放火	058
防災無線	054
法事	028
ボーナス	019, 129, 135
保証会社	046
保証人	047
母乳	032
ボランティア	061, 092, 187

ポリープ	040
ホワイトデー	081-082
本	182-183
盆踊り	087

ま

マニュアル車	171
マンション	017, 047, 049-050, 054, 059
万引き	057
マンモグラフィー	041

み

水割り	148
ミニバン	051

め

目覚まし時計	002

も

燃えないゴミ	017-018
燃えるゴミ	017-018
模擬試験	166
木造住宅	057
喪主	073
モップ	016
喪服	073-074
紅葉狩り	098

や

家賃	048, 050, 130
ヤミ金	023

ゆ

有給休暇	118, 130
雪かき	056

よ

養育費	020

容積率	050
浴室乾燥機	013
予算	020
予備校	039, 166
四輪駆動	051

ら

LINE	181
ラッシュ	139

り

離婚	024, 068-070
理髪店	159-160
留学	038, 172-174
流産	031
領収書	022
料理	008-009, 011
旅行保険	023
リンス	004

れ

礼金	048
冷凍	009
レジ袋	010
レントゲン	040

ろ

老眼	043
労災	133
老人ホーム	030, 127
労働組合	118
労働時間	129-130
浪人	039, 176
ロースクール	167
ローン	020, 050-051

わ

ワールドカップ	093-094
ワイシャツ	012
ワクチン	033

《著者紹介》

新崎　隆子（しんざき・りゅうこ）
会議・放送通訳者。東京外国語大学大学院、青山学院大学、玉川大学で教鞭をとる。著書に『これなら通じる！決定版　旅の英会話』（NHK出版）、共著に『英語スピーキング・クリニック』『最強の英語リスニング・実戦ドリル』（研究社）など。

石黒弓美子（いしぐろ・ゆみこ）
会議・放送通訳者。東京外国語大学、立教大学大学院、清泉女子大学で非常勤講師を務める。共著に『英語スピーキング・クリニック』『最強の英語リスニング・実戦ドリル』『英語リスニング・クリニック』（研究社）など。

英語で雑談できるようになる生活フレーズ集

2016年8月1日　初版発行

著　者	新崎　隆子 石黒弓美子
発行者	関戸雅男
印刷所	研究社印刷株式会社
発行所	株式会社　研究社 〒102-8152　東京都千代田区富士見2-11-3 電話　営業 03-3288-7777(代)　編集 03-3288-7711(代) 振替　00150-9-26710 http://www.kenkyusha.co.jp/

KENKYUSHA
〈検印省略〉

装　丁	株式会社イオック（目崎智子）
本文デザイン・組版・イラスト	株式会社インフォルム
英文校閲	Kathryn A. Craft
編集協力	望月羔子、市川しのぶ、三島知子

© Ryuko Shinzaki and Yumiko Ishiguro, 2016
ISBN978-4-327-44111-1　C1082　Printed in Japan